The Spirit And The Word

A Treatise on the Holy Spirit in the Light of a Rational Interpretation of the Word of Truth

by
Z.T. Sweeney

ISBN 1-58427-067-5

Guardian of Truth Foundation
P.O. Box 9670
Bowling Green, Kentucky 42102

TABLE OF CONTENTS

TABLE OF CONTENTS

INTRODUCTION

CHRISTIANITY is differentiated from all the other religions by the fact that it offers its followers a spiritual dynamic in living up to its precepts. That dynamic is the Holy Spirit, that sets the word of God on fire, warms the church from coldness to enthusiasm, and strengthens the Christian with a power not his own in the great battle between the flesh and the spirit.

Christianity is unique in making this offer. No other religion has any equivalent for it. The Holy Spirit is not obtained from the deductions of logic, the conclusions of philosophy nor from the investigations of science. All these are as silent as the grave regarding his presence and potency.

It is solely and distinctly a matter of divine revelation. It is not my purpose, therefore, to view this subject in the light of philosophic induction, logical deduction nor scientific investigation, but solely in the light of God's revelation. I shall gather the teaching of God's word around several important phases of the nature, mission and work of the Spirit. I do not speculate upon what God may do through his Spirit; I put no limit upon the power of the Spirit. He may work in a thousand ways, for aught I know. I am treating solely of that work of the Spirit which God has made plain in his revealed word.

For the sake of simplifying the treatment of the subject, I shall use the words "Spirit" and "Holy Spirit" instead of other terms used in the Scriptures. The Old Testament has eighty-eight distinct references to the Holy Spirit. In these references there are eighteen names applied. The New Testament refers to the Spirit two hundred and sixty-four times and uses thirty-nine names. Five names are common to both Testaments, which leaves fifty-two different appellatives for the Spirit. Seventeen appellatives express his relation to God, five his relation to the Son, five indicate his divine nature, seven describe his own character, while seventeen are used to indicate his relation to man. He is called the Holy Spirit, the Spirit of God, the Spirit of Christ, the Spirit of Jesus, the Spirit of his Son, of the Lord, of Truth, of Grace, of Holiness, of Glory, and of Adoption. He is called the Comforter, but this term never denotes his relation to man in general. It always describes a special relation to the apostles and their work.

I wish my readers to bring to the perusal of this work the same spirit of earnestness that I shall put into the task of producing it. We read in the language of Jesus that "every sin and blasphemy shall be forgiven unto men; but the blasphemy against the Spirit shall not be forgiven" (Matt. 12:31). "And every one who shall speak a word against the Son of man, it shall be forgiven him: but unto him that blasphemeth against the Holy Spirit it shall not be forgiven" (Luke 12:10).

Whatever else these terrible warnings may teach, they undoubtedly teach that the greatest care should be taken by those who venture to discuss this subject or investigate such discussion. Let both writer and reader therefore cast aside any flippancy of spirit, also any preconceptions or prejudices, and say like young Samuel of old: "Speak, Lord; thy servant heareth."

The subject may be made plain or simple according to the manner we may treat it. If we view it in the light of psychological manifestations in our own hearts, or in the lives of those around us, which are ascribed to the Spirit, we shall find ourselves wandering in a maze of mystery. If we follow the word of God, which is the only source of knowledge, we shall find ourselves walking in a light that shall grow brighter as we proceed. It is impossible in a book the size of this to treat all the many passages that refer to the Holy Spirit, but we shall give those that have important bearing upon the subject.

I

THE SPIRIT AND THE OLD TESTAMENT

THE Old Testament does not give the same prominence to the Holy Spirit as does the New Testament. This is doubtless true because the Old Testament deals largely with material things, while the New Testament is primarily and essentially dealing with the spiritual nature and actions of man. It is, however, referred to in more than half of the books of the Old Testament, while in sixteen of them there is no specific mention of the Spirit. It is, however, mentioned specifically eighty-eight times in the Old Testament. It is generally spoken of as the Spirit of God. The New Testament refers to these passages in such a way as to identify the Holy Spirit of the New with the Spirit of God of the Old. In Luke 4:18 Jesus says:

"The Spirit of the Lord is upon me,
Because he anointed me to preach good
  tidings to the poor:
He hath sent me to proclaim release to
  the captives,
And recovering of sight to the blind.
To set at liberty them that are bruised,
To proclaim the acceptable year of the
  Lord."

This is directly connected with the "Spirit of the Lord Jehovah" in Isa. 61: 1, 2.

In the second chapter of Acts we have a direct connection with Joel 2. These are two of many such connections that bind together and identify the Spirit of the Lord of the Old Testament with the Holy Spirit of the New. In both Testaments we find God working by his Spirit. The Old Testament gives three lines of work performed by the Spirit:

1. HIS RELATION TO THE MATERIAL UNIVERSE.

(1) In Gen. 1: 2 we are told: "And the Spirit of God moved on the face of the waters." The word "moved" carries the sense of "hovered" or "brooded."

The previous condition of the world was "waste and void," or a "formless waste." In some way the Spirit of God fashioned this formless waste into the multiplicity of contrasts that followed. It bound together those elements that were homogeneous, and separated the heterogeneous and so prepared the way for the dividing the light from the darkness that followed. The mode of the operation we do not know, but the fact of the operation is clearly revealed.

(2) "By his Spirit the heavens are garnished" (Job 26:13). The expression could be better translated, "The heavens are made fair," or beautiful. That is, he set the constellations in their order. He gives one illustration when he says: "His hand hath pierced the swift serpent." Reference is here made to the beautiful constellation of "Serpens," or Draco, of graceful and striking appearance.

(3) God's Spirit made me man; 'twas the Almighty's breath that gave me life. This higher life that was given to man by an inbreathing of the Spirit distin-

11

guishes man (*homo*) from all other animal species.

2. THE RELATION OF THE SPIRIT TO CREATED MAN.

(1) Gen. 6:3. God tells Noah: "My Spirit shall not strive with man for ever, for that he also is flesh: yet shall his days be a hundred and twenty years." Here the work of the Spirit passes from the form of omnipotence to one of pleading or striving. The Spirit no more impresses his will upon the material universe, but expresses (rolls it out) to a rational creature. By the preaching of the faithful Noah the Spirit plead with the antediluvians to do right and escape the destruction that was coming upon a corrupt and wicked world. From this time onward the Spirit comes on men in various ways, qualifying them with supernatural power for the performance of special duties.(See Num. 11: 25; Judg. 3: 10; 1 Sam. 18: 10; 10: 11.)

(2) But we find no case of the Spirit falling on man to cleanse him from sin, or to confer upon him a special blessing. Later on in the prophets the Spirit be-

comes a revealing and inspiring Spirit. (See Isa. 61:1; Ezek. 2:2; Zech. 7:12; 4: 6.) As a result of this revealing power, we have the great facts of the New Testament set forth in detail. The life, nature, character and mission of the world's Redeemer stand forth in beauty and symmetry.

3. THE RELATION OF THE SPIRIT TO THE INDIVIDUAL MAN.

The idea of holiness is not usually associated with the Spirit in the Old Testament. The term "Holy Spirit" occurs but three times in it. David prays (Ps. 51:11): "Take not thy holy Spirit from me." Isaiah says (63:10): "They rebelled and grieved his holy Spirit;" and again (63:11) he asks: "Where is he that put his holy Spirit in the midst of them?" It is, however, called "good Spirit" twice (Neh. 9:20; Ps. 143:10).

It is mainly in reference to Messianic days that we find this ethical and personal relation to the Spirit of God.

These three relations of the Spirit are in perfect harmony with God's law of progressive development in the world.

We find him at first working upon a chaotic material universe; second, upon society, and, third, upon the individual character.

The work of the Spirit upon the material universe makes it a fit dwelling-place for man. His work upon society makes man fit to dwell in the universe, and his work upon the individual character makes man fit for a righteous and holy fellowship with similar characters.

II

THE SPIRIT AND THE NEW TESTAMENT

THERE are two hundred and sixty-four references to the Spirit in the New Testament. But in many of them there is no allusion to the Holy Spirit. In many places the expressions "the Spirit," and "the Holy Spirit," should be rendered "Spirit" and "holy Spirit," or frequently "a holy Spirit." The passages in this chapter are arranged in two columns: Column 1 contains the passages in which the definite article is to be found in the Greek. These should always be translated "the Holy Spirit." Column 2 contains the passages where the definite article is not found and which may be often—but not always—translated "a holy Spirit." The use of the article is often governed by other parts of speech. Where the Spirit sustains a universal relation to mankind, the word is italicized.

15

THE SPIRIT AND THE WORD

MATTHEW.

3: 16. He saw the Spirit of God descending as a dove, and coming upon him.

4: 1. Then was Jesus led up of the Spirit into the wilderness to be tempted of the devil.

10: 20. For it is not ye that speak, but the Spirit of your Father that speaketh in you.

12: 18. I will put my Spirit upon him.

12: 31. The blasphemy against the Spirit shall not be forgiven.

12: 32. Whosoever shall speak against the Holy Spirit, it shall not be forgiven him.

28: 19. Baptizing them into the name of the Father and of the Son and of the Holy Spirit.

1: 18. She was found with child of the Holy Spirit.

1: 20. That which is conceived in her is of the Holy Spirit.

3: 11. He shall baptize you in the Holy Spirit, and in fire.

12: 28. If I by the Spirit of God cast out demons.

22: 43. How then doth David in the Spirit call him Lord.

MARK.

1: 10. Coming up out of the water, he saw . . . the Spirit as a

1: 8. He shall baptize you in the Holy Spirit.

16

d o v e descending upon him.

1: 12. Straightway t h e Spirit driveth him forth into the wilderness.

3: 29. Whosoever s h a l l blaspheme against the Holy Spirit hath never forgiveness.

12: 36. David himself said in the Holy Spirit.

13: 11. It is not ye that speak, but the Holy Spirit.

LUKE.

2: 26. It had been revealed unto him by the Holy Spirit.

2: 27. He came in the Spirit into the temple.

3: 22. The Holy Spirit descended in a bodily form, as a dove, upon him.

4: 1. Jesus . . . was led in the Spirit in the wilderness.

4: 14. Jesus returned in the power of the Spirit into Galilee.

4: 1. Jesus, full of the Holy Spirit, re-

1: 15. He shall be filled with [the] H o l y Spirit.

1: 35. [The] Holy Spirit shall come upon thee.

1: 41. Elisabeth w a s filled w i t h [the] Holy Spirit.

1: 67. Zacharias w a s filled w i t h [the] Holy Spirit.

2: 25. There was a man in J e r u s a l e m, whose name was Simeon; . . . [the] Holy Spirit was upon him.

turned from the Jordan.

12: 10. Unto him that blasphemeth against the Holy Spirit it shall not be forgiven.

12: 12. The Holy Spirit shall teach you in that very hour what ye ought to say.

24: 49. Behold, I send forth the promise of my Father upon you.

3: 16. He shall baptize you in [the] Holy Spirit and in fire.

4: 18. The Spirit of the Lord is upon me.

10: 21. He rejoiced in [the] Holy *Spirit*.

11: 13. How much more shall your heavenly Father give [the] *Holy Spirit* to them that ask him?

JOHN.

1: 32. I have beheld the Spirit descending as a dove out of heaven; and it abode upon him.

1: 33. Upon whomsoever thou shalt see the Spirit descending, and abiding upon him.

3: 6. That which is born of the Spirit is spirit.

3: 8. So is every one that is born of the Spirit.

3: 34. He giveth not the Spirit by measure.

6: 63. It is the spirit that giveth life.

1: 33. The same is he that baptizeth in the Holy Spirit.

3: 5. Except one be born of water and [the] *Spirit*.

7: 39. [The] Spirit was not yet given.

20: 22. He breathed on them, and saith unto them, Receive ye [the] Holy Spirit.

7: 39. This spake he of the Spirit, which they t h a t believed on him were to receive.

14: 16. He shall give you another Comforter.

14: 17. Even the Spirit of truth.

14: 26. The Comforter, even the Holy Spirit, ... he shall teach you.

15: 26. When the Comforter is come, . . . even the Spirit of truth, . . . he shall bear witness of me.

16: 7. If I go not away, the Comforter will not come unto you.

16: 8. He, when he is come, will convict the world in respect of sin, and of righteousness, a n d of judgment.

16: 9. Of sin, because they believe not on me;

16: 10. O f righteousness, because I go to the Father;

16: 11. Of judgment, because the prince of this world h a t h been judged.

19

16: 13. When he, the Spirit of truth, is come, he shall guide you into all the truth: for he shall not speak from himself; but what things soever he shall hear, these shall he speak: and he shall declare unto you the things that are to come.

16: 14. He shall glorify me: for he shall take of mine, and shall declare it unto you.

16: 15. He taketh of mine, and shall declare it unto you.

ACTS.

1: 4. He charged them ... to wait for the promise of the Father.

1: 8. Ye shall receive power, when the Holy Spirit is come upon you.

1: 16. The scripture should be fulfilled, which the Holy Spirit spake before by the mouth of David concerning Judas.

1: 2. He had given commandment through [the] Holy Spirit unto the apostles.

1: 5. John indeed baptized with water; but ye shall be baptized in [the] Holy Spirit.

2: 4. They were all filled with the Holy Spirit, and began to speak with

20

2: 17. I will pour forth of my Spirit upon all flesh:

2: 18. On my servants and on my handmaidens in those days will I pour forth my Spirit.

2: 33. Having received of the Father the promise of the Holy Spirit, he hath poured forth this.

2: 38. Ye shall receive the gift of the Holy Spirit.

4: 25. Who by the Holy Spirit, by the mouth of our father David, . . . didst say.

4: 31. They were all filled with the Holy Spirit, and they spake the word of God with boldness.

5: 3. Why hath Satan filled thy heart to lie to the Holy Spirit.

5: 9. How is it that ye have agreed together to try the Spirit of the Lord?

5: 32. We are witnesses of these things;

other tongues, as [the] Spirit gave them utterance.

4: 8. Peter, filled with [the] Holy Spirit, said unto them.

6: 3. Look ye out . . . seven men . . . full of [the] *Spirit*.

6: 5. Stephen, a man full of . . . the Holy *Spirit*.

7: 55. He, being full of [the] Holy *Spirit*.

8: 15. Who . . . prayed for them, that they might receive [the] Holy Spirit.

8: 16. For as yet it was fallen upon none of them.

8: 17. Then laid they their hands on them, and they received [the] Holy Spirit.

8: 19. Give me also this power, that on whomsoever I lay my hands, he may receive [the] Holy Spirit.

8: 39. [The] Spirit of the Lord caught away Philip.

and so is the Holy Spirit.

6: 10. They were not able to withstand . . . the Spirit by which he spake.

7: 51. Ye do always resist the Holy Spirit.

8: 18. When Simon saw that through the laying on of the apostles' hands the Holy Spirit was given,

8: 20. Thou hast thought to obtain the gift of God with money.

8: 29. The Spirit said unto Philip, Go near, and join thyself to this chariot.

9: 31. The c h u r c h . . . walking . . . in the comfort of the Holy Spirit, was multiplied.

10: 19. The Spirit said unto him, Behold, three men seek thee.

10: 20. Go with them. . . . I have sent them.

10: 44. The Holy Spirit fell on all them that heard the word.

10: 45. On the Gentiles also was poured out the

9: 17. Jesus . . . hath sent me, that thou mayest . . . be filled with [the] Holy Spirit.

10: 38. God anointed him with [the] Holy Spirit and with power.

11: 16. Ye shall be baptized in [the] Holy Spirit.

11: 24. He was a good man, and full of [the] Holy Spirit.

13: 9. Paul, filled with [the] Holy Spirit, fastened his eyes on him.

13: 52. The disciples were filled with joy and with [the] Holy Spirit.

19: 2. Did ye receive [the] Holy Spirit when ye believed? . . . We did not so much as h e a r whether [the] Holy Spirit was given.

gift of the Holy
Spirit.

10: 47. Who have received
the Holy Spirit as
well as we?

11: 12. The Spirit bade me
go with them.

11: 25. As I began to speak,
the Holy Spirit fell
on them.

11: 28. Agabus . . . signi-
fied by the Spirit
that there should be
a great famine over
all the world.

13: 2. The Holy Spirit
said, Separate me
Barnabas and Saul.

13: 4. They, being sent
forth by the Holy
Spirit.

15: 8. God . . . bare them
witness, giving them
the Holy Spirit.

15: 28. It seemed good to
the Holy Spirit, and
to us.

16: 6. Forbidden of the
Holy Spirit, to speak
the word in Asia.

16: 7. The Spirit of Jesus
suffered them not.

19: 6. When Paul had laid
his hands upon

23

them, the Holy
Spirit came on them.

20: 22. I go bound in the
spirit unto Jerusa-
lem.

20: 28. Take heed . . . to
all the flock, in
which the Holy
Spirit hath made
you bishops.

21: 4. These said to Paul
through the Spirit,
that he should not
set foot in Jerusa-
lem.

21: 11. Thus saith the Holy
Spirit, So shall the
Jews at Jerusalem
bind the man that
owneth this girdle.

28: 25. Well spake the Holy
Spirit through Isa-
iah the prophet.

ROMANS.

8: 2. The law of the
Spirit of life in
Christ Jesus made
me free from the law
of sin and of death.

8: 10. The spirit is life
because of right-
eousness.

8: 11. If the Spirit of him
that raised up Jesus

1: 4. Who was declared
to be the Son of
God with power,
according to [the]
spirit of holiness.

5: 5. The love of God
hath been shed
abroad in our
hearts through
[the] Holy *Spirit*.

24

from the dead dwelleth in you, he . . . shall give life also to your mortal bodies through his Spirit.

8: 16. The *Spirit* himself beareth witness with our spirit.

8:23. Who have the first-fruits of the Spirit.

8: 26. The Spirit also helpeth our infirmity: . . . the Spirit himself maketh intercession for us.

8: 27. He . . . knoweth what is the mind of the Spirit.

9: 1. I say the truth . . . my conscience bearing witness with me in the Holy Spirit.

15: 30. I beseech you . . . by the love of the Spirit.

8: 4. The ordinance of the law might be fulfilled in us, who walk . . . after [the] *Spirit*.

8: 5. They that are after [the] *Spirit* the things of [the] *Spirit*.

8: 9. Ye are . . . in the *Spirit,* if . . . [the] Spirit of God dwelleth in you. But if any man hath not the *Spirit* of Christ, he is none of his.

8: 13. If by [the] *Spirit* ye put to death the deeds of the body, ye shall live.

8: 14. As many as are led by [the] *Spirit* of God, these are the sons of God.

8:15. Ye received [the] *spirit* of adoption.

14: 17. The kingdom of God is . . . righteousness and peace and joy in [the] Holy *Spirit*.

15: 13. That ye may abound in hope, in

THE SPIRIT AND THE WORD

the power of [the]
Holy *Spirit*.

15: 16. The offering up of
the Gentiles might
be m a d e accept-
able, being sancti-
fied by [the] Holy
Spirit.

15: 19. In the power of
[the] Holy Spirit.

1 CORINTHIANS.

2: 10. God revealed them
through the Spirit;
for the S p i r i t
searcheth all things.

2: 11. The things of God
none knoweth, save
the Spirit of God.

2: 12. But we received . . .
the spirit which is
from God.

2: 14. The n a t u r a l man
receiveth n o t t h e
things of the Spirit
of God.

3: 16. Know ye not . . .
that the Spirit of
God d w e l l e t h in
you?

6: 11. Ye w e r e justified
. . . in the Spirit of
our God.

6: 19. Your body is a temple of the Holy
Spirit.

2: 4. My speech and my
preaching were . . .
in demonstration
of [the] Spirit.

2: 13. In w o r d s . . .
which [the] Spirit
teacheth.

7: 40. I think that I also
have [the] spirit of
God.

12: 3. No man speaking
in the Spirit of
God saith, Jesus is
anathema; and no
man can say, Jesus
is Lord, but in
[the] Holy Spirit.

14: 2. In [the] Spirit he
speaketh mysteries.

12: 4. There are diversities of gifts, but the same Spirit.

12: 7. To each one is given the manifestation of the Spirit to profit withal.

12: 8. To one is given through t h e Spirit the word of wisdom; and to another the word of knowledge, according to t h e same Spirit.

12: 9. To another faith, in the s a m e Spirit; and to another gifts of healings, in the one Spirit.

12: 11. All t h e s e worketh the one and the same Spirit, dividing to each one severally even as he will.

2 CORINTHIANS.

1: 22. Who . . . gave us the earnest of the Spirit in our hearts.

3: 6. The letter killeth, but the spirit giveth life.

3: 8. How shall not rather the ministration of

3: 3. Ye are an epistle of Christ, . . . written . . . with [the] *Spirit* of the living God.

3: 18. We all . . . are transformed i n t o the s a m e image

27

the spirit be with glory?

4: 13. Having the same spirit of faith.

5: 5. Who gave unto us the earnest of the Spirit.

12: 18. Walked we not in the same Spirit?

13: 14. The communion of the Holy Spirit, be with you all.

from glory to glory, even as from the Lord [the] Spirit.

6: 6. In kindness, in [the] Holy *Spirit*, in love unfeigned.

11: 4. If ye receive a different *spirit*, which ye did not receive.

GALATIANS.

3: 2. Received ye the Spirit by the works of the law, or by the hearing of faith?

3: 5. He . . . that supplieth to you the Spirit.

3: 14. That we might receive the promise of the *Spirit* through faith.

4: 6. God sent forth the *Spirit* of his Son into our hearts.

5: 17. The flesh lusteth against the *Spirit*, and the *Spirit* against the flesh.

5: 22. The fruit of the *Spirit* is love, joy, peace.

3: 3. Having begun in [the] *Spirit*, are ye now perfected in the flesh?

4: 29. He that was born after the flesh persecuted him that was born after [the] *Spirit*.

5: 5. We through [the] *Spirit* by faith wait for the hope of righteousness.

5: 16. Walk by [the] Spirit, and ye shall not fulfil the lust of the flesh.

5: 18. If ye are led by [the] *Spirit*, ye are not under the law.

5: 25. If we live by [the] *Spirit*, by the

28

6: 8. He that soweth un-
to the *Spirit* shall
of the *Spirit* reap
eternal life.

Spirit let us also
walk.

EPHESIANS.

1: 13. Ye were sealed with
the Holy Spirit of
promise.

2: 18. Through h i m we
both have our access
in one Spirit unto
the Father.

3: 16. That ye may be
strengthened w i t h
power through his
Spirit in the inward
man.

4: 3. Keep the unity of
the *Spirit* in the
bond of peace.

4: 4. There is one body,
and one *Spirit*.

4: 30. Grieve not the Holy
Spirit of God, in
w h o m ye w e r e
sealed.

6: 17. Take . . . the swórd
of the Spirit, which
is the word of God.

1: 17. That God . . . may
give unto you a
spirit of wisdom
and revelation in
the knowledge of
him.

2: 22. In whom ye also
are b u i l d e d to-
gether for a habi-
tation of God in
[the] *Spirit*.

3: 5. It hath now been
revealed unto his
holy apostles and
prophets in [the]
Spirit.

5: 18. Be filled with [the]
Spirit.

6: 18. Praying at all sea-
s o n s in [t h e]
Spirit.

PHILIPPIANS.

1: 19. The supply of the
S p i r i t of Jesus
Christ.

2: 1. If there is . . .
any fellowship of
[the] *Spirit*.

29

THE SPIRIT AND THE WORD

3: 3. We are the circumcision, w h o worship by [the] *Spirit* of God.

COLOSSIANS.

1: 8. Who also declared unto us your love in [the] *Spirit*.

1 THESSALONIANS.

4: 8. God, who giveth his Holy S p i r i t unto you.

6: 19. Q u e n c h n o t the *Spirit*.

1: 5. Our gospel came not unto you in word only, but . . . in the Holy Spirit.

1: 6. Having received the word . . . with joy of [the] Holy *Spirit*.

2 THESSALONIANS.

2: 13. God chose you . . . in sanctification of [the] *Spirit*.

1 TIMOTHY.

4: 1. The Spirit saith expressly, that . . . some shall fall away from the faith.

4: 14. Neglect not the gift that is in thee.

3: 16. He who was . . . justified in [the] spirit.

2 TIMOTHY.

1: 7. God gave us not a spirit of fearfulness; but of power and love and discipline.

1: 14. That g o o d thing . . . guard through [the] Holy Spirit.

TITUS.

3: 5. H e s a v e d u s through the . . . renewing of [the] Holy *Spirit*.

HEBREWS.

3: 7. Wherefore, even as the H o l y Spirit saith, To-day if ye will hear his voice.

4: 3. Even as he hath said.

4: 7. He again defineth a certain day.

9: 8. The H o l y Spirit this signifying.

10: 15. The H o l y Spirit also beareth witness to us.

10: 29. Hath done despite unto the *Spirit* of grace?

2: 4. God also bearing witness with them, . . . by gifts of [the] Holy Spirit.

6: 4. Were made partakers of [the] Holy Spirit.

9: 14. Who through [the] eternal Spirit offered himself without blemish unto God.

JAMES.

4: 5. Doth the *S p i r i t* which he made to dwell in us long unto envying?

THE SPIRIT AND THE WORD

1 PETER.

1: 11. Searching what time . . . the Spirit of Christ . . . did point unto.

3: 18. Put to death in the flesh, but made alive in the spirit.

4: 14. The Spirit of glory and the Spirit of God resteth upon you.

1: 2. In sanctification of [the] *Spirit*.

1: 12. Preached the gospel unto you in [the] Holy Spirit.

4: 6. Live according to God in [the] spirit.

2 PETER.

1: 21. Men spake from God, being moved by [t h e] H o l y Spirit.

1 JOHN.

2: 20. Ye have an anointing from the Holy One.

2: 27. The anointing which ye received of him abideth in you.

3: 24. We know that he abideth in us by the Spirit which he gave us.

4: 2. Hereby know ye the S p i r i t of G o d: Every spirit that c o n f e s s e t h that Jesus Christ is come in the flesh is of God.

4: 6. By this we know the spirit of truth, and the spirit of error.

4: 13. He hath given us of his Spirit.

5: 7. It is the Spirit that beareth witness, because the Spirit is the truth.

5: 8. There are three who bear witness, the S p i r i t, and t h e water, and the blood.

JUDE.

19. Having not [the] *Spirit*.

20. Praying in [the] Holy *Spirit*.

REVELATION.

1: 4. The seven Spirits that are before his throne.

2: 7. H e a r w h a t t h e Spirit saith to the churches.

2: 17. H e a r w h a t t h e Spirit saith to the churches.

2: 29. H e a r w h a t t h e Spirit saith to the churches.

3: 1. He that hath the seven Spirits of God.

1: 10. I was in [the] *S p i r i t* o n t h e Lord's day.

4: 2. Straightway I was in [the] *Spirit*.

11: 11. The breath of life from God entered into them.

17: 3. He c a r r i e d me a w a y in [t h e] *Spirit* into a wilderness.

21: 10. He c a r r i e d me a w a y in [t h e]

3 33

3: 6.   Hear w h a t the Spirit saith to the churches.

3: 13. Hear w h a t the Spirit saith to the churches.

:4 5.   Seven lamps of fire . . . which are the s e v e n Spirits of God.

5: 6.   S e v e n eyes, which are the seven Spirits of God.

14: 13. Yea, saith the Spirit, that they may rest from their labors.

22: 17. The Spirit and the bride say, Come, *Spirit* to a mountain.

III

THE PERSONALITY AND DIVINITY OF THE SPIRIT

TWO views have been entertained concerning the Holy Spirit: (1) That it is a divine influence proceeding from the Father, an emanation from or manifestation of the divine, or a mere impersonal force. (2) That he is a person and active in all the ways of a personality. That the latter view is the correct and Scriptural one is evident from the following considerations:

1. HIS WORKS PROCLAIM PERSONALITY.

(1) *He speaks.* "But the Spirit saith expressly, that in later times some shall fall away from the faith" (1 Tim. 4:1). A speaker is a person; no influence or principle can speak.

(2) *He testifies.* "But when the Comforter is come, whom I will send unto you from the Father, even the Spirit of

truth, which proceedeth from the Father, he shall bear witness of me'' (John 15: 26).

(3) *He teaches and quickens the mind.* "But the Comforter, even the Holy Spirit, whom the Father will send in my name, he shall teach you all things, and bring to your remembrance all that I said unto you'' (John 14:26).

(4) *He guides.* "I have yet many things to say unto you, but ye can not bear them now. Howbeit when he, the Spirit of truth, is come, he shall guide you into all the truth'' (John 16: 12, 13).

(5) *He leads and forbids.* "And they went through the region of Phrygia and Galatia, having been forbidden of the Holy Spirit to speak the word in Asia; and when they were come over against Mysia, they assayed to go into Bithynia; and the Spirit of Jesus suffered them not'' (Acts 16:6, 7).

(6) *He searches.* "But unto us God revealed them through the Spirit: for the Spirit searcheth all things, yea, the deep things of God'' (1 Cor. 2:10).

In the above passages the Holy Spirit is said to speak, to testify, to quicken, to teach, to guide disciples, to lead, to forbid and to search. All these things unite in showing the Holy Spirit to be a person, for nothing but a person can do them.

2. HE HAS THE CHARACTERISTICS OF A PERSON. We will mention a few of them:

(1) *Mind.* "And he that searcheth the hearts knoweth what is the *mind of the Spirit*" (Rom. 8:27).

(2) *Knowledge.* "Even so the things of God none knoweth, save the Spirit of God" (1 Cor. 2:11).

(3) *Affection.* "Now I beseech you, brethren, by our Lord Jesus Christ, and by the *love of the Spirit*, that ye strive together with me in your prayers to God for me" (Rom. 15:30).

(4) *Will.* "But all these worketh the one and the same Spirit, dividing to each one severally even *as he will*" (1 Cor. 12:11).

(5) *Goodness.* "Thou gavest also thy *good Spirit* to instruct them" (Neh. 9:

20). Goodness, will, affection, knowledge and mind are all characteristics of a person. By no stretch of the imagination can they be ascribed to a mere impersonal influence or principle. These five characteristics form the fingers in the hand of certainty by which we grasp the personality of the Holy Spirit.

3. HE SUFFERS SLIGHTS AND INJURIES THAT CAN ONLY BE ASCRIBED TO A PERSONALITY.

(1) *He can be grieved and vexed.* "And grieve not the Holy Spirit of God, in whom ye were sealed unto the day of redemption" (Eph. 4: 30). "But they rebelled, and grieved his holy Spirit: therefore he was turned to be their enemy, and himself fought against them" (Isa. 63: 10).

(2) *He can be despited.* "Of how much sorer punishment, think ye, shall he be judged worthy, who hath trodden under foot the Son of God, and hath counted the blood of the covenant wherewith he was sanctified an unholy thing, and hath *done despite* unto the Spirit of grace" (Heb. 10: 29).

(3) *He can be blasphemed.* "Therefore I say unto you, Every sin and blasphemy shall be forgiven unto men; but the blasphemy against the Spirit shall not be forgiven. And whosoever shall speak a word against the Son of man, it shall be forgiven him; but whosoever shall speak against the Holy Spirit, it shall not be forgiven him, neither in this world, nor in that which is to come" (Matt. 12:31, 32).

(4) *He can be resisted.* "Ye stiffnecked and uncircumcised in heart and ears, ye do always resist the Holy Spirit" (Acts 7:51).

(5) *He can be lied unto.* "But Peter said, Ananias, why hath Satan filled thy heart to lie to the Holy Spirit, and to keep back part of the price of the land?" (Acts 5:3).

A mere principle can not sustain any of the above slights. Nothing but a personality can be blasphemed, lied to, resisted or grieved.

4. HE IS A DIVINE PERSONALITY. This will be seen from the following attributes, which are the attributes of God:

THE SPIRIT AND THE WORD

(1) *Eternity.* "How much more shall the blood of Christ, who through the *eternal* Spirit offered himself without blemish unto God, cleanse your conscience from dead works to serve the living God?" (Heb. 9:14). "Jehovah is great in Zion; And he is high above all the peoples" (Ps. 99:2).

(2) *Omniscience.* "But unto us God revealed them through the Spirit: for the Spirit *searcheth all things,* yea, the deep things of God. For who among men knoweth the things of a man, save the spirit of the man, which is in him? even so the things of God none knoweth, save the Spirit of God" (1 Cor. 2:10, 11).

(3) *Omnipotence.* "But as for me, I am full of power *by the Spirit* of Jehovah, and of judgment, and of might, to declare unto Jacob his transgression, and to Israel his sin" (Mic. 3:8).

(4) *Omnipresence.* "Whither shall I go from thy Spirit? Or whither shall I flee from thy presence? . . . Even there shall thy hand lead me, And thy right hand shall hold me" (Ps. 139:7, 10). "Can any hide himself in secret places so

that I shall not see him? saith Jehovah. Do not I fill heaven and earth? saith Jehovah'' (Jer. 23:24).

5. THE WORKS OF THE HOLY SPIRIT MANIFEST DIVINITY.

(1) The work of *creation*. "And the earth was waste and void; and darkness was upon the face of the deep: and the Spirit of God moved upon the face of the waters'' (Gen. 1:2). "By his Spirit the heavens are garnished; his hand hath pierced the swift serpent'' (Job 26:13). "By the word of Jehovah were the heavens made, And all the host of them by the breath of his mouth'' (Ps. 33:6). "The Spirit of God hath made me, And the breath of the Almighty giveth me life'' (Job 33:4).

(2) The work of *providence*. "Thou sendest forth thy Spirit, they are created; and thou renewest the face of the ground'' (Ps. 104:30).

(3) The work of *regeneration* and resurrection. "Jesus answered, Verily, verily, I say unto thee, Except one be born of water and the Spirit, he cannot enter into the kingdom of God'' (John

3:5). "But if the Spirit of him that raised up Jesus from the dead dwelleth in you, he that raised up Christ Jesus from the dead shall give life also to your mortal bodies through his Spirit that dwelleth in you" (Rom. 8:11).

(4) He is the source of the *miraculous*. "But if I by the Spirit of God cast out demons, then is the kingdom of God come upon you" (Matt. 12:28). "To another faith, in the same Spirit; and to another gifts of healing, in the one Spirit; . . . but all these worketh the one and the same Spirit, dividing to each one severally even as he will" (1 Cor. 12:9, 11).

Thus in his works, his characteristics, the things he suffers, his attributes and his achievements, we have a fivefold cord of testimony that clearly demonstrates the Spirit's personality and divinity.

IV

THE SPIRIT AND JOHN THE BAPTIST

THE first mention of the Holy Spirit in the New Testament is in connection with John the Baptist: "There was in the days of Herod, king of Judæa, a certain priest named Zacharias, of the course of Abijah: and he had a wife of the daughters of Aaron, and her name was Elisabeth. And they were both righteous before God, walking in all the commandments and ordinances of the Lord blameless" (Luke 1:5, 6).

This Zacharias was taking his turn in the temple service, and an angel appeared unto him and announced that in answer to his prayer his wife Elisabeth should bear a son whose name should be called John; that he should be great, and should drink no wine nor strong drink, and (Luke 1:15) "he shall be filled with the Holy Spirit, even from his mother's womb"; and "his father Zacharias was *filled with the Holy Spirit,* and prophesied, saying, Blessed be the Lord, the God of Israel; for he hath visited and wrought redemption for his people" (Luke 1:67, 68).

And the child John grew and "waxed strong in spirit, and was in the deserts till the day of his showing unto Israel" (Luke 1:80). His private life was spent in the desert solitudes, where he was being strengthened in spirit for the great work God had prepared for him. This work had been foretold by the Holy Spirit. It spake through Isaiah the prophet (40:3), saying: "The voice of one that crieth, Prepare ye in the wilderness the way of Jehovah; make level in the desert a highway for our God. Every valley shall be exalted, and every mountain and hill shall be made low; and the rough places a plain: and the glory of Jehovah shall be revealed, and all flesh shall see it together." Again, Malachi (3:1) says: "Behold, I send my messenger, and he shall prepare the way before me."

In fulfillment of these predictions of the Spirit came John the Baptist in the fifteenth year of the reign of Tiberius Cæsar, preaching the baptism of repentance for the remission of sins. Great multitudes flocked to his preaching and baptism. Among others came Jesus of Nazareth, and "on the morrow he seeth Jesus coming unto him, and saith, Behold, the Lamb of God, that taketh away the sin of the world" (John 1:29). "This is he of whom I said, After me cometh a man who is become before me: for he was before me. And I knew him not; but that he should be made manifest to Israel, for this cause came I baptizing in water. And John bare witness, saying, I have beheld the Spirit descending as a dove out of heaven; and it abode upon him. And I knew him not: but he that sent me to baptize in water, he said unto me, Upon whomsoever thou shalt see the Spirit descending, and abiding upon him, the same is he that baptizeth in the Holy Spirit. And I have seen, and have borne witness that this is the Son of God" (John 1:30-34).

THE SPIRIT AND THE WORD

The next mention of the Holy Spirit by John the Baptist is in reference to the baptism in the Holy Spirit and in fire. In order that the reader may have a clear understanding of this disputed and difficult subject, I shall present the testimonies of the four Evangelists in parallel columns:

MATT. 3: 10-12.

And even now the axe lieth at the root of the trees: every tree therefore that bringeth not forth good fruit is hewn down, and cast into the fire. I indeed baptize you in water unto repentance: but he that cometh after me is mightier than I, whose shoes I am not worthy to bear: he shall baptize you in the Holy Spirit and in fire: whose fan is in his hand, and he will thoroughly cleanse his threshing-floor; and he will gather his wheat into the garner, but the chaff he will burn up with unquenchable fire.

MARK 1: 7, 8.

And he preached, saying, There cometh after me he that is mightier than I, the latchet of whose shoes I am not worthy to stoop down and unloose. I baptize you in water; but he shall baptize you in the Holy Spirit.

LUKE 3: 9, 16, 17.

And even now the axe also lieth at the root of the

JOHN 1: 33.

And I knew him not: but he that sent me to

trees: every tree therefore that bringeth not forth good fruit is hewn down, and cast into the fire. . . . John answered, saying unto them all, I indeed baptize you in water; but there cometh he that is mightier than I, the latchet of whose shoes I am not worthy to unloose; he shall baptize you in the Holy Spirit and in fire: whose fan is in his hand, thoroughly to cleanse his threshing - floor a n d to gather the wheat into his garner; but the chaff he will burn up with unquenchable fire. baptize in water, he said unto me, Upon whomsoever thou shalt see the Spirit descending, and abiding upon him, the same is he that baptizeth in the Holy Spirit.

John is preaching to a mixed multitude composed of those who would accept his teaching and baptism, and of those who would accept neither. Many of the former would become disciples of Jesus and receive the baptism of the Holy Spirit to qualify them to take up the work of the Master and carry it on until the church would be established and the gospel fully revealed to men. The baptism of the Spirit, a purely supernatural thing, was necessary to qualify them for this work.

Others would "reject for themselves the counsel of God, being not baptized of him." These should at last "have their part in the lake that burneth with fire and brimstone." That such a division was meant by John becomes evident if we examine the context carefully. In the above parallel columns the reader will observe that Matthew and Luke use the expression "in the Holy Spirit and in fire." They both use two illustrations to show what is meant by "in fire." One of the illustrations immediately precedes and the other immediately follows the expression "in the Holy Spirit and in fire," seemingly for the specific purpose of guarding against a failure to understand the expression "in fire." The illustration that precedes in both instances is: "Therefore every tree that bringeth not forth good fruit is hewn down and cast into the fire." The illustration that follows in each instance is: "He will burn up the chaff in unquenchable fire." With these forcible illustrations to guard the passage, can any one fail to understand what is meant by the baptism in fire? The reader will also observe that neither Mark nor John refers to the baptism in fire, and neither uses any illustration to explain it, because no illustration is necessary. Where the baptism of fire is used there was always something destroyed by fire. This interpretation harmonizes with the universal use of the word "fire" in the New Testament. (1) *In not a single instance is it used to denote a spiritual blessing conferred upon the good.* (2) *In not a single instance does it refer to the work of the Holy Spirit in purifying sinners.* It is connected with judgments, punishments, fiery indignation, devouring adversaries, consuming, and even with hell itself; but in no case does it refer to the power of God in the scheme of redemption to convert and save men.

Neither does the baptism of the Holy Spirit refer to cleansing men from sin and saving them. *It was not given for that purpose.* This is a foolish dream born out of the castaway doctrine of the total depravity of man and his total disability to hear, believe and obey the truth.

Those who claim the baptism of the Holy Spirit to-day claim that it is the regenerating, converting, purifying power of God. *But the Bible does not so teach.* In every instance in which the word "purify" is found in the New Testament it is an act of personal volition—*something a man must do for himself.* John 11:55: "Now the passover of the Jews was at hand: and many went up to Jerusalem out of the country before the passover, to purify themselves."

Acts 21:24: "These take, and purify thyself with them, and be at charges for them, that they may shave their heads; and all shall know that there is no truth in the things whereof they have been informed concerning thee; but that thou thyself also walkest orderly, keeping the law."

Acts 21:26: "Then Paul took the men, and the next day purifying himself with them went into the temple, declaring the fulfilment of the days of purification, until the offering was offered for every one of them."

Jas. 4:8: "Draw nigh to God, and he will draw nigh to you. Cleanse your hands, ye sinners; and purify your hearts, ye doubleminded.''

1 Pet. 1:22: Seeing ye have purified your souls in your obedience to the truth unto unfeigned love of the brethren, love one another from the heart fervently.''

1 John 3:3: ''And every one that hath this hope set on him purifieth himself, even as he is pure.''

''Men must cleanse themselves from wrong in thought, word and deed, and purify their souls in obeying the truth. The Bible teaches that this is God's way of purifying sinners'' (*H. R. Pritchard,* ''*Addresses,*'' p. 323).

From this chapter the reader will obtain the following Scripture facts:

1. The Holy Spirit rested on John the Baptist from his mother's womb.

2. The Holy Spirit filled his father Zacharias so that he prophesied.

3. The Holy Spirit bore witness to Jesus by descending and abiding upon him, enabling John to identify him.

4. John promised a baptism in the Holy Spirit to some of his auditors and threatened others with a baptism in fire.

THE SPIRIT AND THE WORD

1 Pet. 1:11, 12: "Searching what time or what manner of time the Spirit of Christ which was in them did point unto, when it testified beforehand the sufferings of Christ, and the glories that should follow them. To whom it was revealed, that not unto themselves, but unto you, did they minister these things, which now have been announced unto you through them that preached the gospel unto you by the Holy Spirit sent forth from heaven: which things angels desire to look into."

V

THE SPIRIT AND JESUS

THE relation sustained by the Holy Spirit to Jesus Christ is a twofold one. First: He predicted by the holy prophets the great facts in the life of the coming one. Second: He associated himself with that one after he came.

1. THE TIME OF HIS COMING WAS CLEARLY FORETOLD. He was to come "in the last days," or in the end of the Jewish Dispensation. "And it shall come to pass in the latter days, that the mountain of Jehovah's house shall be established on the top of the mountains, and shall be exalted above the hills; and all nations shall flow unto it" (Isa. 2:2).

2. HE WAS TO COME WHILE THE SECOND TEMPLE WAS IN EXISTENCE. "Behold, I send my messenger, and he shall prepare the way before me: and the Lord, whom ye seek, will suddenly come *to his temple*;

and the messenger of the covenant, whom ye desire, behold, he cometh, saith Jehovah of hosts" (Mal. 3:1).

3. THE PLACE OF HIS NATIVITY WAS A MATTER OF PROPHECY. "But thou, Bethlehem Ephrathah, which art little to be among the thousands of Judah, out of thee shall one come forth unto me that is to be ruler in Israel; whose goings forth are from of old, from everlasting" (Mic. 5:2).

4. HIS LINEAGE WAS DECLARED IN THE JEWISH SCRIPTURES.

(1) *He was to be a descendant of Abraham.* "In thee shall all the families of the earth be blessed" (Gen. 12:3). "For verily not of angels doth he take hold, but he taketh hold of the seed of Abraham" (Heb. 2:16).

(2) *He was to be of the tribe of Judah.* "For it is evident that our Lord hath sprung out of Judah; as to which tribe Moses spake nothing concerning priests" (Heb. 7:14).

(3) *He was to be of the house of David.* "And it shall come to pass in that day, that the root of Jesse, which

standeth for an ensign of the peoples, unto him shall the nations seek; and his resting-place shall be glorious" (Isa. 11:10).

5. HIS CHARACTER WAS MINUTELY DESCRIBED BY THE PROPHETS.

(1) *His wisdom.* "And the Spirit of Jehovah shall rest upon him, the spirit of wisdom and understanding, the spirit of counsel and might, the spirit of knowledge and of the fear of Jehovah" (Isa. 11:2).

(2) *His obedience.* "For I am come down from heaven, not to do mine own will, but the will of him that sent me" (John 6:38).

(3) *His love of righteousness.* "Thou hast loved righteousness, and hated wickedness: Therefore God, thy God, hath anointed thee with the oil of gladness above thy fellows" (Ps. 45:7).

(4) *His gentleness and tenderness.* "He will not cry, nor lift up his voice, nor cause it to be heard in the street. A bruised reed will he not break, and a dimly burning wick will he not quench: he will bring forth justice in truth" (Isa. 42:2, 3).

(5) *His compassion.* "The Spirit of the Lord Jehovah is upon me; because Jehovah hath anointed me to preach good tidings unto the meek; he hath sent me to bind up the broken-hearted, to proclaim liberty to the captives, and the opening of the prison to them that are bound" (Isa. 61:1).

6. HIS BETRAYAL AND TRIAL. As we approach the closing scenes of Christ's life the prophecies become more minute and remarkable.

(1) *The betrayal.* "And I said unto them, If ye think good, give me my hire; and if not, forbear. So they weighed for my hire thirty pieces of silver. And Jehovah said unto me, Cast it unto the potter, the goodly price that I was prized at by them. And I took the thirty pieces of silver, and cast them unto the potter, in the house of Jehovah" (Zech. 11:12, 13).

(2) *His demeanor when on trial.* "He was oppressed, yet when he was afflicted he opened not his mouth; as a lamb that is led to the slaughter, and as a sheep

that before its shearers is dumb, so he opened not his mouth" (Isa. 53:7).

(3) *When crucified, the soldiers were to part his garments among them and cast lots for his vesture.* "They part my garments among them, And upon my vesture do they cast lots" (Ps. 22:18).

(4) *He was to be numbered with the transgressors.* "Therefore will I divide him a portion with the great, and he shall divide the spoil with the strong; because he poured out his soul unto death, and was numbered with the transgressors; yet he bare the sin of many, and made intercession for the transgressors" (Isa. 53:12).

(5) *He was to perish amid cruel mockings.* "But I am a worm, and no man; a reproach of men, and despised of the people. All they that see me laugh me to scorn: they shoot out the lip, they shake the head, saying, Commit thyself unto Jehovah; let him deliver him: let him rescue him, seeing he delighted in him" (Ps. 22:6-8).

7. His Resurrection and Coronation.

(1) *He was to rise from the dead.* "For thou wilt not leave my soul to

Sheol; neither wilt thou suffer thy holy one to see corruption" (Ps. 16:10).

(2) *His ascension was also a subject of prophecy.* "Thou hast ascended on high, thou hast led away captives; thou hast received gifts among men, yea, among the rebellious also, that Jehovah God might dwell with them" (Ps. 68:18).

(3) *His coronation is foretold and described.* "I saw in the night visions, and, behold, there came with the clouds of heaven one like unto a son of man, and he came even to the ancient of days, and they brought him near before him. And there was given him dominion, and glory, and a kingdom, that all the peoples, nations, and languages should serve him: his dominion is an everlasting dominion, which shall not pass away, and his kingdom that which shall not be destroyed" (Dan. 7:13, 14).

The above are only a few of the many predictions made by the Holy Spirit as to the character, life, sacrifice and dominion of our Lord. We notice now the work of the Spirit in, upon and through him.

THE SPIRIT AND JESUS

1. HE WAS CONCEIVED BY THE HOLY
SPIRIT. "Now the birth of Jesus Christ
was on this wise: When his mother Mary
had been betrothed to Joseph, before
they came together she was found with
child of the Holy Spirit" (Matt. 1:
18). "And the angel answered and said
unto her, The Holy Spirit shall come
upon thee, and the power of the Most
High shall overshadow thee: wherefore
also the holy thing which is begotten shall
be called the Son of God" (Luke 1:35).

2. HE WAS ANOINTED BY THE HOLY
SPIRIT. "And Jesus, when he was baptized, went up straightway from the
water: and lo, the heavens were opened
unto him and he saw the Spirit of God
descending as a dove, and coming upon
him; and lo, a voice out of the heavens,
saying, This is my beloved Son, in whom
I am well pleased" (Matt. 3:16, 17).
"And it came to pass in those days, that
Jesus came from Nazareth of Galilee, and
was baptized of John in the Jordan. And
straightway coming up out of the water,
he saw the heavens rent asunder, and the
Spirit as a dove descending upon him:

and a voice came out of the heavens, Thou art my beloved Son, in thee I am well pleased'' (Mark 1:9-11). ''Now it came to pass, when all the people were baptized, that, Jesus also having been baptized, and praying, the heaven was opened, and the Holy Spirit descended in a bodily form, as a dove, upon him, and a voice came out of heaven, Thou art my beloved Son; in thee I am well pleased'' (Luke 3:21, 22). ''And John bare witness, saying, I have beheld the Spirit descending as a dove out of heaven; and it abode upon him, and I knew him not: but he that sent me to baptize in water, he said unto me, Upon whomsoever thou shalt see the Spirit descending, and abiding upon him, the same is he that baptizeth in the Holy Spirit'' (John 1: 32, 33).

3. HE WAS LED BY THE HOLY SPIRIT. ''Then was Jesus led up of the Spirit into the wilderness to be tempted of the devil'' (Matt. 4:1). ''And straightway the Spirit driveth him forth into the wilderness'' (Mark 1:12). ''And Jesus, full of the Holy Spirit, returned from the

Jordan, and was led in the Spirit in the wilderness'' (Luke 4:1).

4. HE WROUGHT MIRACLES BY THE HOLY SPIRIT. ''But if I by the Spirit of God cast out demons, then is the kingdom of God come upon you'' (Matt. 12:28). ''But if I by the finger of God cast out demons, then is the kingdom of God come upon you'' (Luke 11:20).

5. HE OFFERED HIMSELF UP THROUGH THE HOLY SPIRIT. ''How much more shall the blood of Christ, who through the eternal Spirit offered himself without blemish unto God, cleanse your conscience from dead works to serve the living God?'' (Heb. 9:14).

6. HE WAS RAISED BY THE HOLY SPIRIT. ''But if the Spirit of him that raised up Jesus from the dead dwelleth in you, he that raised up Christ Jesus from the dead shall give life also to your mortal bodies through his Spirit that dwelleth in you'' (Rom. 8:11). ''Who was declared to be the Son of God with power, according to the spirit of holiness, by the resurrection from the dead'' (Rom. 1:4).

7. HE GAVE THE COMMISSION BY THE
HOLY SPIRIT. "The former treatise I
made, O Theophilus, concerning all that
Jesus began both to do and to teach,
until the day in which he was received
up, after that he had given commandment
through the Holy Spirit unto the apostles whom he had chosen" (Acts 1:1, 2).

8. HIS ASCENSION AND CORONATION
WERE ANNOUNCED BY THE HOLY SPIRIT.
"Being therefore by the right hand of
God exalted, and having received of the
Father the promise of the Holy Spirit,
he hath poured forth this, which you see
and hear" (Acts 2:33). "Let all the
house of Israel therefore know assuredly,
that God hath made him both Lord and
Christ, this Jesus whom ye crucified"
(Acts 2:36).

Thus the Spirit predicted the coming
of Jesus and the great facts of his birth,
baptism, anointing, miracles, death, burial
and resurrection, ascension and coronation, and then came from the Father to
carry on the work of extending his kingdom. In the light of this testimony we
can truly say with Paul in 2 Cor. 12:3:

"Wherefore I make known unto you, that no man speaking in the Spirit of God saith, Jesus is anathema: and no man can say, Jesus is Lord, *but in the Holy Spirit.*"

"I manifested thy name unto the men whom thou gavest me out of the world: thine they were, and thou gavest them to me; and they have kept thy word. Now they know that all things whatsoever thou hast given me are from thee: for the words which thou gavest me I have given unto them; and they received them, and know of a truth that I came forth from thee, and they believe that thou didst send me. . . . While I was with them, I kept them in thy name which thou hast given me: and I guarded them, and not one of them perished, but the son of perdition; that the scripture might be fulfilled. . . . I have given them thy word; and the world hated them, because they are not of the world, even as I am not of the world. I pray not that thou shouldst take them from the world, but that thou shouldst keep them from the evil one" (John 17: 6-8, 12, 14, 15).

VI

THE SPIRIT AND THE APOSTLES

IN interpreting Scripture, attention should be paid not only to the speaker and his message, but also to the parties addressed. There are passages that are universal in their application, others that are national, and still others that are addressed to individuals only. Many promises are addressed to children of God only, and do not apply to those who are not citizens of Christ's kingdom. Again, there are commands that are addressed solely to men in a state of condemnation, and have no relevancy when applied to the children of God. Christ uttered many things to his chosen ambassadors, chosen to establish his kingdom on earth, which were never intended to be applied to any others. It is a mistake for the Christian of to-day to make *universal,* promises that were intended by our Lord for special individuals. It confuses the whole scheme of redemption and makes a mystery out of Scriptures that are perfectly clear when proper limitations are made. Things addressed to a chosen few have been wrongly applied to all and great confusion has resulted therefrom. It is my purpose in this chapter to notice some of these.

The fourteenth, fifteenth and sixteenth chapters of John contain a record of a private talk by our Lord to the twelve, and to *them alone.* Jesus was approaching the close of his earthly ministry. He had chosen his apostles, and they had left all to follow him. He had eaten, slept and companied with them. He had taught them the great truths upon which his kingdom would be founded. They had learned to depend upon him for advice, instruction, comfort and guidance. They confessed this when they said, "Thou hast the words of eternal life."

He was soon to leave them, and knew that they would feel that they were "as sheep without a shepherd." He wishes them to know that they should not be left orphaned. He tells them, "I will pray the Father, and he shall give you *another* Comforter that he may abide with you for ever," or to the remotest age. That is, as long as you shall have need of him. The Greek word translated "for ever" does not necessarily mean unlimited duration. It is often applied to much shorter periods, even to a lifetime.

The word "Comforter" is a translation from the Greek word *Paracletos,* and it is a very inadequate translation. There is no word within my knowledge that will fully express in English the Greek word. It is much better to Anglicize the word into the English "Paraclete." This word is used of the Holy Spirit only four times in the New Testament, and is only used by the Saviour in his private address to the twelve, found in the fourteenth, fifteenth and sixteenth chapters of John. It is never applied to the work of the Holy Spirit in relation to mankind in general. It is promised only to the chosen, and Jesus tells them that *the world* can not receive "him."

This Paraclete is a distinct gift to the twelve, to take the place of the personal presence and guidance of the leader who is preparing to leave them.

What is the nature of this promised one? By examining the lexicons we find that Paraclete is

1. One called or sent to assist another.

2. One who pleads the cause of another.

3. A monitor.

4. An instructor.

5. A guide.

6. A helper.

7. A supporter.

8. A comforter.

Of this Paraclete Jesus says:

1. Whom the world *can not receive.*

2. He dwelleth with *you* and shall be in *you.*

3. He shall teach *you* all things.

4. He shall bring all things to *your* remembrance whatsoever I have spoken unto *you.*

5. He shall testify of me.

6. He shall convict the world of sin.

7. He shall convict the world of right-eousness.

8. He shall convict the world of judgment.

9. He shall guide *you* into all truth.

10. He shall show *you* things to come.

11. He shall receive of mine and show it *unto you*.

Here we have eleven distinct things that the Paraclete is to do for the apostles.

All these offices of the Paraclete were needed by the apostles in their work of proclaiming Christianity and establishing the church. They were ignorant and unlearned, humanly speaking, and could never have gone forth to success without this supernatural Paraclete. They took no thought what they should say, for it was given them at the proper time. Others have to take thought. Paul tells Timothy to "study to show thyself approved unto God, a workman that needeth not to be ashamed, rightly dividing the word of truth." Timothy had to study because he did not possess the Paraclete. Yet Timothy did possess the gift of the Spirit. "For which cause I put thee in remembrance that thou stir up the gift of God, which is in thee through the laying on of my hands" (2 Tim. 1: 6).

Men to-day are required to study that they may know what to say. A failure to observe this exhortation of the apostle is the reason why a great many do not know what to say. The Paraclete was not only an instructor, but he was an infallible guide. This is evident from the fact that no apostle ever contradicted another nor said anything foolish. I never heard a man of to-day lay claim to being guided "into all truth by the Spirit," who did not say something foolish in the next five minutes. If any man claims the direct guidance of the Spirit to-day, he can not consistently deny that same claim to others. But we have all sorts of men teaching all sorts of doctrines, often contradicting each other. Does the Spirit guide one man to preach up Universalism and another man to preach it down? The same is true of Calvinism, Mormonism or any other ism.

This teaching places the Spirit in a very unenviable position, that of preaching four or five different teachings at the same time, each within a half-mile of the other. Suppose a preacher were to do that? What would the people think of him? It would ruin the reputation of any preacher in Christendom. There is something wrong, and that something is *to apply to the world* the promise of the Paraclete, which was *only given to the apostles.*

Paul tells Timothy: "The things thou hast heard of me among many witnesses, the same commit thou to faithful men who shall be able to teach others also." Was that not an impertinence in Paul if Timothy had the same divine leading as he? Was it not impertinence in Jude to say that the faith was "once for all delivered to the saints," if there were deliverances being constantly made? What need to preach the gospel to the heathen world if God is directly leading men into all truth? What need for a New Testament if all men possess this Paraclete? How can one man deny the claims of another whom he admits to be divinely guided into all truth?

Some have thought that Christ bestowed the Paraclete upon the apostles when he breathed upon them and said: "Receive ye the Holy Spirit." At best that was a prophetic and not an actual bestowal, for after that onbreathing we find Peter (Acts 1) calling upon the assembly of brethren to *take a vote* as to who should succeed Judas in the apostolic college. If he had possessed the Paraclete at that time, he would not have been compelled to resort to the judgment of his brethren to determine such a question. Moreover, Christ indicated when the Paraclete would come, by stating the work that would follow his coming: *"When he is come* he shall convict the world [age] of sin, of righteousness and of judgment." How did he do this?

1. His first act at his coming was to baptize the apostles in the Spirit and endow them with the Paraclete. "Ye shall be baptized in the Holy Spirit not many days hence" (Acts 1:5).

2. When the Spirit baptized these apostles with divine guidance he began

his work of convicting the world through them.

(1) *To convict the world of sin.* Not of sin in general. It is a mistaken idea that the Spirit is sent to personally convict a man of the sin of lying, stealing or defrauding his neighbor. When I was a boy in old Kentucky the colored people used to hold great revivals; they generally selected corn-planting-time or harvest-time for these meetings. Many of them would lie for days in a cataleptic condition, which, they said, was a "conviction of the Spirit." A man would go groaning and moping to his task because he was "under conviction of the Holy Ghost." The above passage teaches nothing of the kind, nor does any other passage in the New Testament teach it. There is not a case in the New Testament where the Holy Spirit ever made an issue with a man to personally convict him of sin. All men are convicted of sin by the Spirit, but it is the Spirit working through the preaching of Spirit-filled men. "And he, when he is come, will convict the world [the Jewish world or

age] in respect of sin, because they *believe not on me.*" They called him a blasphemer, they rejected him, they took him with wicked hands and crucified and slew him; and the first thrust of the Spirit on the day of Pentecost was at this sinful act of the world: "This same Jesus whom ye took with wicked hands and crucified and slew, God hath raised him up and made him both Lord and Christ."

(2) *"Of righteousness, because I go to the Father, and ye behold me no more."* If this passage teaches that men are individually convicted of sin, it also teaches that they are individually convicted of righteousness, and this would be a most herculean task, even for the Spirit, to perform. It is a contradiction of terms to say that the Spirit convicts a man of sin, then, in the next breath, that he convicts the same man of righteousness. And yet, the Spirit was to convict men "of righteousness"; but whose righteousness? *The righteousness of Jesus Christ.* "Of righteousness, because I go to the Father, and ye behold me no more." When Jesus

74

was on earth he claimed to be the Son of God; he claimed to come down from heaven; he claimed to be God manifest in the flesh; but, at the same time, he was a "man of sorrows and acquainted with grief." "There was no beauty that we should desire him." On this account the Jews refused to accept him as the Son of God; they denied his claim to divinity and called him a blasphemer for making himself equal with God; they believed that he was unrighteous in making that claim, and Jesus died because his claims were not accepted by his people; but after his death he was crowned with glory and honor at the right hand of the Majesty on high, and the Spirit came to demonstrate the righteous claims Jesus made while on earth. The Spirit came to convict men of the righteousness of Christ, and not their own righteousness. A simple illustration will probably throw light upon this thought. Forty years ago my father lived in a little village in the State of Illinois, midway between St. Louis and Indianapolis. One afternoon two young lads, covered with dust and

toilworn, came to his house and told him
they were sons of an elder of a Christian
Church in Indiana; that they had been
robbed in St. Louis, and were making
their way home on foot; they asked for
something to eat. My father doubted
their claims; he felt that they were im-
postors; but my mother, who had boys of
her own out in the world, and who always
believed the best of everybody, said: "We
will feed them and care for them during
the night." Their wants were supplied,
and they were given lodging for the night,
and sent on their way the next morning
with a good lunch for the day. Six
months afterward, I preached in Monroe
County, Indiana, and, stopping with one
of the elders of the church, two young
lads were introduced to me as his boys.
They asked me if my father lived in
Illinois. I told them he did. They then
recounted their experience at my father's
home, and said to me: "We would be glad
when you return home if you will tell
your father that you stopped at our
house, and that you know we were what
we claimed to be when we sought his

aid." When I returned to my father's home I convicted him of the righteousness of those boys in the claim which they set forth, and which he had hitherto doubted. In a similar manner the Spirit of God came down to convict the world, that had rejected the claims of Jesus, of his righteousness in making those claims.

(3) *He will convict the world of judgment, because the "prince of this world is judged."* This passage does not say, as many preachers quote it, "of judgment *to come,*" but "of judgment, because the prince of this world is judged." This Scripture is often quoted to show that a judgment was pronounced upon Satan, who is often called the prince of this world. The word for prince in the original is used thirty-seven times—thirty-two times it clearly means an earthly ruler, and five times it may apply to Satan. There is no reason why the expression, "the prince of this world," may not mean an earthly ruler. It evidently refers to Pontius Pilate, in John 14: 30, when Jesus says: "The prince of this

world cometh, and he hath nothing in me." Pilate justifies that statement when he says: "I find no fault in this man." Nevertheless, as prince of this world, he pronounced the death-sentence and delivered him up to be crucified. This was the judgment of the prince of this world, but the descent of the Holy Spirit on the day of Pentecost reversed this judgment and pronounced a righteous judgment in its place, thus judging Pilate "the prince of this world." The above three things were accomplished on the day of Pentecost by the coming of the Spirit. The Jews were convicted of sin in rejecting and crucifying Christ; they were also convicted of the righteousness of Christ in claiming to be the Son of God, and likewise convinced that God had raised up Jesus and made him both Lord and Christ. In accomplishing this work the Spirit did it through the instrumentality of gospel preaching, and all subsequent convictions of sin, of righteousness and of judgment have been accomplished through the same agency, and will be till the end of time.

This Paraclete continued with the apostles till the end of their ministry, guiding, leading, and showing them "things to come," bringing all things to their remembrance that Christ had spoken unto them. Under this direct a d supernatural control they preached the gospel to all the nations of the earth, and established the church with all its officers, ordinances, privileges and duties. They wrote the epistles to the churches and gave to mankind the New Testament, "the perfect law of liberty." The work of the Paraclete being finished, and his mission ended, no man has been guided, shown and directed personally by him since. God does no unnecessary work, and the work of the Paraclete is not necessary now. His work remains in the teachings and lives of the apostles. There are many things in the abovementioned chapters that rightfully have a universal application, but the special promises concerning the Paraclete are not included in those things.

THE SPIRIT AND THE WORD

"Wherefore he saith, When he ascended on high, he led captivity captive, And gave gifts unto men. . . . And he gave some to be apostles; and some, prophets; and some, evangelists; and some, pastors and teachers; for the perfecting of the saints, unto the work of ministering, unto the building up of the body of Christ: till we all attain unto the unity of the faith, and of the knowledge of the Son of God, unto a fullgrown man, unto the measure of the stature of the fulness of Christ" (Eph. 4:8, 11-13).

VII

THE SPIRIT AND THE APOSTOLIC CHURCH

THAT the Holy Spirit sustained a relation to the apostolic church that it does not sustain to the church of to-day is clearly evident to the student of the Divine Word. The church of the apostolic age had no New Testament as we have to-day. Hence the necessity of a more direct and immediate leading than is necessary to-day. The apostle Paul states the difference between the two when he says: "For we know in part, and we prophesy in part; but when that which is perfect is come, that which is in part shall be done away." This is not a contrast between the imperfections of our day and the perfection of heaven, but between the imperfection of the apostolic church and the perfection of the church of to-day. That which is perfect *has come;* a perfect

6 81

revelation of Christian character, a perfect gospel, a perfect "law of liberty," a perfect New Testament. The apostolic church was limited to knowing *in part* and prophesying *in part*. "But to each one is given the manifestation of the Spirit to profit withal. For to one is given through the Spirit the word of wisdom; and to another the word of knowledge, according to the same Spirit: to another faith, in the same Spirit; to another gifts of healings, in the one Spirit; and to another workings of miracles; and to another prophecy; and to another discernings of spirits: to another divers kinds of tongues; and to another the interpretation of tongues: but all these worketh the one and the same Spirit, dividing to each one severally even as he will" (1 Cor. 12:7-11).

Now, here was manifestly a condition in the first churches that does not exist to-day. Here are various direct and supernatural workings that are manifestations of spiritual power resulting from a direct *gift of the Spirit* to members of apostolic churches. Now, there was a purpose to be accomplished by this special gift of the Spirit. In the fourth chapter of Ephesians the apostle tells us the purpose of this gift. "And he gave some, apostles; and some, prophets; and some, evangelists; and some, pastors and teachers; *for* the perfecting of the saints, *for* the work of the ministry, *for* the edifying of the body of Christ: *Till we all come to the unity of the faith, and of the knowledge of the Son of God."* This gift of the Spirit accompanied the baptism of the Spirit on the day of Pentecost.

This brings us to a very ·interesting question; viz., Was the promise of the "gift of the Holy Spirit," referred to by Peter on the day of Pentecost, a universal one to all who obey the gospel, or was it limited to those of the apostolic church who received it that they might manifest it in a supernatural way "to profit withal," or to the profit of all?

There are some who claim that "the gift of the Spirit" is one that belongs to all who obey the gospel to-day, that it is independent of the instrumentality of the gospel, and is the peculiar heritage of those who repent and are baptized for the remission of sins; that it performs a work in them other than is performed by the Spirit operating through the truth. There are others who claim that the "gift of the Spirit" was a supernatural power and was conferred on persons to qualify them to do a work or works peculiar to the age of miracles which obtained in the apostolic church. The only way to settle this is by appealing to (1) the consciousness of individuals, (2) to the Divine Word.

Before appealing to either of these tribunals, there are a few facts that we must consider. (1) *This is the only passage in the New Testament that connects "the gift of the Spirit" with obedience to the gospel in the preaching of the apostles.* We have remission of sins so connected on various occasions (see Acts 5:31; 10:43; 13:38; 26:18, etc., etc.), but nowhere else is this "gift of the Spirit" promised. If it is to be as universal as "remission of sins," ought it not to have the same prominence in apostolic preaching? This is an important factor in settling the matter. (2) In the only instance in which it is promised it is inexorably connected with *baptism for the remission of sins.* It is promised to no others, and all others are ruled out by the explicit terms of the promise.

With these facts before us, let us now *appeal to the consciousness of the individual.* If we consider numbers, it is safe to say that ninety-five per cent. of those who to-day claim "the gift of the Spirit" have never been baptized for the remission of sins. *They have never performed the conditions upon which the gift was bestowed.* Are they competent to testify? Of the remaining five per cent., there is not one who can give any definite reason why he is *conscious* of the personal indwelling of the Spirit within him. To demonstrate my statement I appeal to the consciousness of my readers. Are you *conscious* of any influence within you except a holy joy that comes from obedience to the will of God? If you are not, what evidence have you that the Spirit personally dwells in you? So much for the argument from consciousness.

THE SPIRIT AND THE WORD

Now let us appeal to the Divine Word.
When the apostle Peter promised "the
gift of the Spirit," he followed it with
the words, *"For the promise* is to you
and to your children, and to all them that
are afar off, even as many as the Lord
our God shall call." He distinctly states
that the gift of the Spirit is in fulfillment
of "the promise." Now, is there in the
Scripture any promise of a personal indwelling of the Holy Spirit as a *result
of obedience?* Let us search the words of
the Master. In Luke 11:13 our Lord
says: "If ye then, being evil, know how
to give good gifts unto your children, how
much more shall your heavenly Father
give the Holy Spirit to them that ask
him?" This passage may be disposed of
by saying that in the original it is *a
holy spirit* and does not refer to *the Holy
Spirit* at all. It represents God's willing-
ness to give *a holy disposition.* Matthew
explains it in the words "good gifts to
them that ask him." In John 7:38, 39
we have recorded another promise: "He
that believeth on me, as the scripture
hath said, from within him shall flow

rivers of living water. But this spake he of the Spirit, which they that believed on him were to receive: for the Spirit was not yet given; because Jesus was not yet glorified.'' This is evidently a supernatural gift, as he represents the recipient of it as a fountain from which flows rivers of living water. This is obviously not true of us to-day. Our Saviour also dates the bestowal as following his glorification, or on the day of Pentecost. In Mark 16:16-18: ''He that believeth and is baptized shall be saved; but he that disbelieveth shall be condemned. And these signs shall accompany them that believe: in my name shall they cast out demons; they shall speak with new tongues; they shall take up serpents, and if they drink any deadly thing, it shall in no wise hurt them; they shall lay hands on the sick, and they shall recover.'' These five things that accompanied the believers are all supernatural. Of the three promises of Jesus—which are all that are recorded in the New Testament—only two refer to the Holy Spirit, and both of these to its *supernatural manifestation.*

87

THE SPIRIT AND THE WORD

If we go back of the Saviour to the Old Testament, we find a distinct promise of the gift of the Spirit: "And it shall come to pass afterward, that I will pour out my Spirit upon all flesh; and your sons and your daughters shall prophesy, your old men shall dream dreams, your young men shall see visions: and also upon the servants and upon the hand-maids in those days will I pour out my Spirit" (Joel 2:28, 29). This promise is the one quoted by Peter to explain the manifestations on the day of Pentecost to the people drawn together by that wonderful event. From it he delivers by the Spirit a sermon on the claims of our Lord. He shows that they had taken the Lord by wicked hands and had crucified and slain him; that God had raised him from the dead and had exalted him to his right hand; had given him the *promise of the Holy Spirit;* that what they *saw* and *heard* was the fulfillment of Joel's promise. This promise was not simply to the apostles, for we read in the preceding chapter that the apostles, and the women and Mary the mother of Jesus, and his brethren to the number of one hundred and twenty all continued with one accord in prayer and supplication. "And when the day of Pentecost was now come, they were all together in one place. And suddenly there came from heaven a sound as of the rushing of a mighty wind, and it filled all the house where they were sitting. And there appeared unto them tongues parting asunder, like as of fire; and it sat upon *each of them.* And they *were all filled* with the Holy Spirit, and began *to speak* with other tongues, as the Spirit gave them utterance." This shows that the gift of the Spirit came upon all the followers Jesus left behind him. When the multitude were convicted by the apostle's discourse, they "said unto Peter and the rest of the apostles, Brethren, what shall we do? And Peter said unto them, Repent ye, and be baptized every one of you in the name of Jesus Christ unto the remission of your sins: and ye shall receive the gift of the Holy Spirit. *For to you is the promise,* and to your children, and to all that are afar off, even as many as the Lord our God shall call unto him.'' What promise? Evidently the promise of God, ''I will pour out of my spirit upon all flesh.'' There is no other promise in the mind of Peter and his hearers, and I know of no other promise the reader can have in mind. This position is amply supported by after-developments. ''While Peter yet spake these words, the Holy Spirit fell on all them that *heard the word*. And they of the circumcision that believed were amazed, as many as came with Peter, because that on the Gentiles also was poured out the gift of the Holy Spirit. For they heard them speak with tongues, and magnify God. Then answered Peter, Can any man forbid the water, that these should not be baptized, who have *received the Holy Spirit* as well as we?'' (Acts 10:44-47). This was in fulfillment of the promise not only to the Jews, but the Gentiles, whom the Jews regarded as ''far off.'' Paul, speaking to Gentiles, says: ''But now in Christ Jesus, ye that were once far off are made nigh in the blood of Christ'' (Eph. 2:13). In this incident ''the gift of the Holy Spirit'' and "receiving the Spirit" are the same. And when Peter was taken to task for baptizing the Gentiles, he defends himself on the ground that God, who knows the heart, bore witness to them, *giving them the Holy Spirit, "the like gift as he did also unto us."* In the above instances, Pentecost and the house of Cornelius, the gift of the Spirit was the result of the baptism of the Spirit, the baptism of the Spirit was an outpouring or falling of the Spirit upon the Jews at Pentecost and the Gentiles at the house of Cornelius, to signify his acceptance of both Jew and Gentile into the kingdom of Christ. Paul undoubtedly refers to this when he says: "For in one Spirit were we all baptized into one body, whether *Jews* or *Greeks*" (1 Cor. 12:13). The baptism of the Spirit ceased when its object—the making of one body out of Jews and Gentiles—was accomplished, but "the gift of the Spirit" did not cease. It was conferred by the laying on of the hands of the apostles through all their lives. A few illustrations may be mentioned from the Scriptures.

THE SPIRIT AND THE WORD

The Samaritans. When a bloody persecution arose at Jerusalem, following the death of Stephen, the disciples were scattered and went everywhere preaching the Word. Philip went to the city of Samaria and preached Christ to them. "But when they believed Philip preaching good tidings concerning the kingdom of God and the name of Jesus Christ, they were baptized, both men and women" (Acts 8:12). "For as yet *the Holy Spirit was fallen upon none of them:* only they had been baptized into the name of the Lord Jesus" (Acts 8:16). If the gift of the Spirit is to all baptized believers, why did not the Samaritans receive it? Philip was not an apostle and did not have the power to confer "the gift of the Spirit" by the imposition of hands, and, in order that they might receive this "gift," it was necessary that two apostles, Peter and John, should go to Samaria and lay hands on them, that they might receive the Spirit. Here is a clear case of baptized believers receiving the Holy Spirit by the imposition of hands.

Disciples at Ephesus. In Acts 19 Paul met certain disciples that had received the baptism of John. He showed them that John did not preach a full gospel, which embraced a belief in Christ. "And when they heard this, they were baptized into the name of the Lord Jesus, and when Paul had *laid his hands upon them,* the Holy Spirit came on them." This is another clear case of the Spirit being given by the imposition of hands.

Timothy. In 2 Tim. 1:6 Paul tells Timothy: "For which cause I put thee in remembrance that thou stir up the gift of God, which is in thee through the *laying on of my hands.*" This is a third instance of the gift of the Spirit by the imposition of hands, and they form just *three more instances* than can be found of the Spirit taking his personal abode in men because they have believed and been baptized.

That the Spirit was imparted to many Christians in a similar way is clear. Paul tells the brethren at Rome: "For I long to see you, that I may impart unto you some *spiritual gift,* to the end that ye may be established." It was not necessary that he see these brethren to the end that he might proclaim the gospel unto them; but it *was necessary* that he see them that he might lay hands on them and *impart the gift* of the Spirit.

In Mark 16:17, 18 Jesus concludes the commission as follows: "And these signs shall accompany them that believe: in my name shall they cast out demons; they shall speak with new tongues; they shall take up serpents, and if they drink any deadly thing, it shall in no wise hurt them; they shall lay hands on the sick, and they shall recover." Here is clearly the promise of supernatural power which he calls "signs." Signs of what? There is but one answer that can be given: signs of the indwelling of God's Spirit by which alone they could work these signs. Are these signs in existence to-day? No thoughtful reader will so affirm. If the manifestations of the Spirit have ceased, is it not reasonable that the "gift" has also ceased? If not, we have the remarkable fact of the Spirit dwelling in man and not being able to *manifest any signs* of his indwelling.

We are now enabled to reach two conclusions of importance: First, the "gift of the Spirit" was a supernatural gift for the purpose of enabling the "believers" in apostolic days to work the "signs" which Christ said should accompany them that believe, and ceased when the signs ceased. Second, many of the exhortations of the New Testament writers were to a church whose members were filled with the supernatural power of the Spirit, and should be interpreted in the light of that fact. We give a few examples that fall under this head: "Declared to be the Son of God with power, according to the spirit of holiness" (Rom. 1:4). "But ye are . . . in the Spirit, if so be that the Spirit of God dwelleth in you" (Rom. 8:9). "Ourselves also, who have the firstfruits of the Spirit" (Rom. 8:23). "My conscience bearing witness with me in the Holy Spirit" (Rom. 9:1). "Now I beseech you, brethren, by our Lord Jesus Christ, and by the love of the Spirit" (Rom. 15:30). "Now he that wrought us for this very thing is God, who gave unto us the earnest of

THE SPIRIT AND THE WORD

the Spirit'' (2 Cor. 5:5). ''Ye were sealed with the Holy Spirit of promise, which is an earnest of our inheritance'' (Eph. 1:13, 14). ''Through him we both have our access in one Spirit unto the Father'' (Eph. 2:18). ''Be filled with the Spirit'' (Eph. 5:18). ''If there is therefore any . . . fellowship of the Spirit'' (Phil. 2:1). ''Therefore he that rejecteth, rejecteth . . . God, who giveth his Holy Spirit unto you'' (1 Thess. 4:8). ''For God gave us not a spirit, of fearfulness; but of power and love and discipline'' (2 Tim. 1:7). ''He saved us through the washing of regeneration and renewing of the Holy Spirit'' (Tit. 3:5). ''God also bearing witness with them, both by signs and wonders and by manifold powers, and by gifts of the Holy Spirit'' (Heb. 2:4). ''Doth the spirit which he made to dwell in us long unto envying?'' (Jas. 4:5). ''Ye have an anointing from the Holy One'' (1 John 2:20). ''The anointing which ye received of him abideth in you'' (1 John 2:27). ''He hath given us of his Spirit'' (1 John 4:13).

All the above Scriptures become clear if we understand them to apply to a people through whom God was manifesting his presence by supernatural demonstrations, but many of them lack meaning when applied to people of God who no longer exhibit these supernatural powers.

VIII

THE SPIRIT AND THE WORLD

HITHERTO we have been treating the Holy Spirit in terms of the past, but now we come to the present tense. Is the Holy Spirit a power in the present age? If so, what kind of a power? Is he making an issue with men as a direct power and working upon them immediately, or is he working through an instrumentality, and, if so, what is the instrumentality?

The Spirit is undoubtedly dealing with two classes of persons in his work to-day.

First, those who are not believers, and therefore unconverted and "aliens from the commonwealth of Israel."

Second, those who have believed and obeyed the gospel, and are therefore children of God.

We shall devote this chapter to the influence of the Spirit upon the unbelieving world.

THE SPIRIT AND THE WORLD

In the very nature of things, the work of the Spirit is to make believers out of unbelievers, and convert the perverted. We all believe this. We believe that all believers are made by the power of the Spirit. We differ about whether he exercises that power directly from himself to the individual soul, or whether he exercises that power through the gospel, through the apostles and through Christ's word of truth. Reason, philosophy and experience exhausted themselves in discovering but two methods by which one spirit can exercise an influence over another.

First, a direct mechanical, immediate influence taking possession of the will and influencing the mind of and controlling the speech and actions of the subject. This takes place in hypnotism and is supposed to take place in clairvoyance and clairaudience.

Second, a rational moral influence exerted by ideas impressed upon the mind by teaching and words that represent ideas.

There is, there can be, no third way by which one spirit can influence another.

You may study till you are gray-headed or bald-headed, for that matter, and you will discover no other way.

The Holy Spirit has used both of these methods in the past.

1. In the case of the apostles and prophets, he immediately, mechanically and directly controlled their actions and speech, so much so that Jesus told them that under the influence of the Spirit they should take no thought what they should say. "For it is not ye that speak, but the Holy Spirit" (Mark 13:11). "And they were all filled with the Holy Spirit, and began to speak with other tongues, as the Spirit gave them utterance" (Acts 2:4).

2. In the case of the men to whom the apostles preached on the day of Pentecost, the Spirit used a rational moral influence through the words of Peter's sermon, which conveyed ideas that swayed their minds and hearts. It is claimed by some that both of these methods are used by the Spirit to-day. The modern teaching concerning the first of these influences is well set forth in the following selection

from a widely known book by L. R. Dunn, entitled "The Mission of the Spirit": "Even where the light of the gospel does not shine, and the institutions of the gospel are not enjoyed, there the Spirit acts directly upon man's heart and conscience, writes the law of God upon his mind, gives him the sense of sin and the need of forgiveness. Hence, wherever man is, there the Comforter is at work upon his heart and mind. The divine influence is imparted *unconditionally* and *irresistibly.* The Holy Spirit is ever employed to bring man back to God; and *whether he desires it or not,* whether he is *willing* or *unwilling,* still the Comforter comes to him with his heavenly illumination, his divine influence, convincing him of sin, and his consequent need of the mercy of God. May I not truly say that man really *has no choice* in the matter as to whether he will or will not have this divine influence upon his soul? *He is, he must be,* enlightened and convinced, *whether he will hear or forbear,* whether he *will be saved or damned.* He *can not prevent* the entrance of the Spirit into his heart."

In connection with the above we quote also from a sermon in "The Baptist Pulpit," by Rev. J. W. Hayhurst: "God has given us no means by which the conversion of sinners, or the general revival of religion, can be effected, irrespective of the *direct* agency of the Spirit. The gospel itself *will not do it.*"

These quotations give us a pretty clear and explicit statement of the theory of the direct mechanical and *immediate* operation of the Holy Spirit upon the human spirit.

The second method is aptly stated by an editorial which appeared in the *Sunday School Times* during the year 1908: "It is a strange fact that, notwithstanding the *explicitness* and *uniformity* of the New Testament teachings on this subject, there is a widespread popular opinion that the Holy Spirit's work is directly and immediately on or in the heart of the unbeliever, without the intervention or agency of the Christian whatever. To hear what is said in the sermons, or sung in the hymns, or prayed in the prayers of many Christians, one might believe that the Holy Spirit is sent directly to the unbelieving sinner, to strive with him, to show him his sin, and to point him to, the Saviour; and that therefore the Christian preacher or teacher has rather to wait the results of this work of the Spirit, than to be the instrument or the avenue of this work. Many a Christian seems to think that the Holy Spirit's work is that of a *revival preacher*, in moving sinners to repentance by a *direct appeal* to their consciences and understandings, instead of stirring up Christians to appeal, in the power of the Spirit, to unbelievers to believe and turn to God. It is true that, in this present dispensation of the Spirit, all power in the evangelizing of the world, and in the swaying of the hearts of men toward Christ and in the service of Christ, is primarily with the Holy Spirit. But it is also true that the Holy Spirit, according to the Bible teachings, works *in and by and through* believers in Jesus. Hence if one who is not a believer in Jesus is to be won to discipleship, the question is not, 'Will the Holy Spirit work on his mind immediately, or will the Holy Spirit work through one who already believes?' for that question *the Bible has already answered.* The Holy Spirit can use the written words, like the spoken words, of a chosen messenger of God to an unbelieving soul. But in every case *the Spirit reaches the believer mediately, not immediately.''*

Now, these theories are directly contradictory. If one is true, the other can not be. The only question to decide is as to which one is true. Let us examine these theories in the light of reason, revelation and experience. If the Holy Spirit works directly and immediately on the heart of man, surely there should be some tangible evidence of it given in such a striking way as to demonstrate the truth of the theory. But the experience of Christendom for nineteen centuries fails to furnish a single unquestioned evidence of it. The proof of the theory is made to hinge upon far-fetched inferences drawn from Scripture statements, and even these fail to furnish the evidence sought. Let us notice some of the Scriptures that are relied upon to prove a direct operation of the Spirit in the conversion of sinners:

1. "A new heart also will I give you, and a new spirit will I put within you; and I will take away the stony heart out of your flesh, and I will give you a heart of flesh. And I will put my Spirit within you, and cause you to walk in my statutes, and ye shall keep mine ordinances, and do them" (Ezek. 36: 26, 27). This passage has been much relied upon to prove the theory of an abstract operation of the Spirit upon the sinner in conversion. Its failure to support the theory is evidenced by the following facts:

(1) The Lord was not talking about the conversion of a sinner, but the renewal of Israel as a people.

(2) The passage says nothing about the work of the Holy Spirit.

(3) There is nothing mentioned in the passage that could not have been accomplished by ordinary means.

(4) The very point to be proven is assumed.

2. "But their minds were hardened: for until this very day at the reading of

the old covenant the same veil remaineth, it not being revealed to them that it is done away in Christ. But unto this day, whensoever Moses is read, a veil lieth upon their heart. But whensoever *it shall turn to the Lord,* the veil is taken away" (2 Cor. 3:14-16). Just what is found here to prove a direct operation of the Spirit would be difficult to say. The apostle is speaking of the Jews reading the Scriptures with a veil which blinds them. The veil was undoubtedly a false interpretation, which prevented their *seeing Christ* in their Scriptures. If they had not this wrong interpretation, they would see Christ and their Scriptures would *be plain.* As it was, they were dark and mysterious. The apostle tells what will remove the veil: *"When they shall turn to the Lord,"* the veil shall be *taken away.* There is nothing in the whole passage that even hints at an immediate operation of the Spirit.

3. "For we are his workmanship, created in Christ Jesus for good works, which God afore prepared that we should walk in them" (Eph. 2:10). There is

nothing here to even hint at a direct operation. It says the Ephesians were created in Christ Jesus (not in the Holy Spirit) unto good works. If the reader wishes to learn by what means they were so created, let him turn to chapter 1, verse 13, and he will obtain the information: "In whom ye also, *having heard* the word of the truth, *the gospel* of your salvation,—in whom, *having also believed,* ye were sealed with the Holy Spirit of promise." That is something to the point. They "heard the word of truth," the gospel of their salvation. Then, *after they believed,* they "were sealed with the Holy Spirit of promise." There is nothing in the passage to warrant the teaching of a special operation to enable them to believe.

4. "And a certain woman named Lydia, a seller of purple, of the city of Thyatira, one that worshipped God, heard us: whose heart the Lord opened to give heed unto the things which were spoken by Paul" (Acts 16:14). This is relied upon to prove a direct work of the Spirit upon Lydia that she might *hear* and *believe.*

107

The very thing to be proved is again assumed. True, the Lord opened Lydia's heart, but he didn't do so that she might "receive the word," for Paul had already preached it to her. Her heart was opened that "she gave heed to the things spoken by Paul." Before she heard Paul she had a narrow, bigoted Jewish heart. After she heard the preaching, her heart was opened to attend to the things she had heard. That is, she obeyed the gospel. Nothing about the Holy Spirit in the entire history.

5. "And I will pray the Father, and he shall give you another Comforter, that he may be with you for ever, even the Spirit of truth: whom the world cannot receive; for it beholdeth him not, neither knoweth him: ye know him; for he abideth with you, and shall be in you" (John 14: 16, 17). As I have elsewhere shown, this passage has a private and peculiar application to the apostles, and not to the world of mankind. It specifically states that "the world cannot receive" this Comforter. That kills it as a proof-text that the world "must receive it" before

it can believe. Those who affirm a direct operation of the Spirit on "the world" make a clear-cut issue with the Saviour.

6. "I planted, Apollos watered; but God gave the increase" (1 Cor. 3:6). Those who use this to prove a special operation of the Spirit make it mean, "I have planted *the word* and Apollos has watered it, but God by a special work of the Holy Spirit makes the increase of the word." This is a false interpretation, as the apostle was not speaking of "the word" at all. How could Apollos *"water the word"?* The apostle was speaking of the *congregation* at Corinth, which he had planted and Apollos had tended, and which, under the care of God, had made increase. There is nothing in the passage about the Holy Spirit.

7. "While Peter yet spake these words, the Holy Spirit fell on all them that heard the word" (Acts 10:44). This has reference to God's signifying his acceptance of the Gentiles by an outpouring similar to the one on the day of Pentecost. It was purely a supernatural act, and has never been repeated since

that day. But even then it would not prove the necessity of an operation of the Spirit, that men might *hear the gospel* and believe it. The record says "it fell on all them that *heard the word*." Cornelius was told by the angel to send for Peter, "who shall tell thee words whereby thou shalt be saved."

8. "Now the natural man receiveth not the things of the Spirit of God: for they are foolishness unto him; and he cannot know them, because they are spiritually judged. But he that is spiritual judgeth all things, and he himself is judged of no man" (1 Cor. 2:14, 15). This is held to be one of the strongest passages to confirm the teaching of the necessity of a direct operation of the Holy Spirit to enable a man to hear and to believe the gospel. A brief examination of the context will show that such an idea was not in the mind of the apostle at all. The apostle is not even speaking of *conversion* when he uses the language. He is speaking of *inspiration*. The spiritual man in Paul's mind was a man inspired by the Spirit, and the natural

110

man was an uninspired man. If the reader will turn to the ninth verse of the chapter and read to the conclusion of the chapter, and place "uninspired" where he finds "natural," and "inspired" where "spiritual" is found, the passage will be as clear as a sunbeam. "The things of the Spirit" are things produced by the Spirit, which needed an inspired man to explain. The day of Pentecost was a "thing of the Spirit," and there was not an uninspired man in all that great throng that could understand it. The best solution they could give was, "These men are drunk," but Peter, an inspired man, explained in inspired language that "this is that which was spoken by the prophet Joel: It shall come to pass in the last days, saith God, that I will pour out of my Spirit upon all flesh." When these natural (uninspired) men heard Peter's (inspired) spiritual explanation, they could understand it. They did understand it and obeyed it to the number of three thousand. Nebuchadnezzar's vision was a "thing of the Spirit," and there was not a natural (uninspired) man

111

in all his realm that could interpret it. But Daniel, a spiritual (inspired) man, explained it in spiritual language and then all could understand it. There is nothing in the passage to support the theory of a direct operation to enable man to understand the gospel.

9. "Him did God exalt with his right hand to be a Prince and a Saviour, to give repentance to Israel, and remission of sins" (Acts 5:31). This passage is used because it speaks of Christ giving repentance. They infer that is done by a direct operation of the Spirit. But the passage says nothing as to *how* he grants repentance. Christ gives many things that are not the result of a direct operation of the Spirit. The very next verse says God gives "the Holy Spirit to all them *that obey* him." This directly contradicts the theory of the necessity of a direct operation of the Spirit to enable men to obey him.

10. "No man can come to me, except the Father that sent me draw him: and I will raise him up in the last day" (John 6:44). This is greatly relied upon to

show the necessity of an irresistible drawing before men can come to Christ. The word "draw," in the Scriptures, is a translation of two words in the original. One means to draw by force, "to drag;" the other means to "entice, allure or persuade"—that men are drawn by moral arguments, or "allured." In the next verse Christ tells how men are drawn. "Every one that hath heard from the Father, and hath learned, cometh unto me." Christ draws men by *"teaching,"* and they come as result of *"learning."* That is why he told his disciples to "go teach all nations." That is Christ's method of drawing.

Now, I have selected ten of the strongest passages in the New Testament that support the theory of a direct operation of the Spirit before men are qualified to hear and obey the gospel. If it is not taught in the above passages, it is not taught in the Bible. When rightly considered, not one of them even leans toward the theory. Are we not justified in saying that the theory is not supported by the Scriptures? Now, how are persons made believers? Hear the word of God:

1. "For I am not ashamed of the gospel: for it is the power of God unto salvation to every one that believeth; to the Jew first, and also to the Greek" (Rom. 1:16). Now, here is the unequivocal statement that God's power to save is lodged in the gospel. In all ages of Christianity there is not a record of a single soul ever being saved without the presence of this power. But this is not a magical power. It must be *heard* in order that it produce faith. But how shall they *hear* without a preacher and how shall he *preach* except he be *sent?* The order is, then, (1) send, (2) preach, (3) hear, (4) believe, (5) obey, (6) saved. Now, this is the order of the Saviour's commission to his followers. "Go preach the gospel to every creature; he that believeth and is baptized shall be saved." That is our marching order to-day.

2. "Now these were more noble than those in Thessalonica, in that they received the word with all readiness of mind, *examining the scriptures* daily,

whether these things were so. *Many of them therefore believed;* also of the Greek women of honorable estate, and of men, not a few" (Acts 17:11, 12). Here were believers made by searching the Scriptures and by receiving the Word with all "readiness of mind." The same method will make believers of unbelievers to-day.

3. "For though ye have ten thousand tutors in Christ, yet have ye not many fathers; for in Christ Jesus I begat you through the gospel" (1 Cor. 4:15). No clearer statement could be made as to the power exercised in begetting men to a new life. They are begotten through the gospel.

4. "Of his own will he brought us forth by the word of truth, that we should be a kind of firstfruits of his creatures" (Jas. 1:18). This is as clear as the one above it. We are brought forth by the Word of truth.

5. "For this people's heart is waxed gross, And their ears are dull of hearing, And their eyes they have closed; Lest haply they should perceive with their eyes, And hear with their ears, And under-

stand with their heart, And should turn again, And I should heal them" (Matt. 13:15). To be healed, one must be converted; to be converted, one must understand with the heart; to understand with the heart, one must perceive and hear. But the people the Lord mentions were not healed. Why? Because they were not converted. Why were they not converted? Because they had not perceived with their eyes and heard with their ears. Why had they not seen and heard? "Their ears are dull of hearing, And their eyes they have closed; Lest at any time they should see with their eyes, And hear with their ears." Men talk of the Bible being a sealed book. They would better talk of sealed *eyes, ears* and *hearts,* as does the Saviour.

IX

THE SPIRIT AND CHRISTIANS

IT has been aptly and truthfully said that "no importance can be attached to a religion that is not begun, carried on and completed by the Spirit of God." That the Christian is led, guided and strengthened by the Spirit can not be denied by any Bible reader. To deny the fact that the Spirit dwells in us is to deny the Bible. But it is asserted with equal clearness in the Divine Word that *God dwells in us.* "And what agreement hath a temple of God with idols? for we are a temple of the living God; even as God said, I will *dwell in them,* and walk in them; and I will be their God, and they shall be my people" (2 Cor. 6:16). This not only says that God will dwell in us, but that he *walks in us.* It is also clearly taught that *Christ dwells in us.* "That Christ may dwell in your hearts

117

through faith; to the end that ye, being
rooted and grounded in love" (Eph.
3:17).

Now, if God, Christ and the Spirit
dwell in us, is there any teaching that the
Spirit dwells in us in a different sense
from that in which the Father and the
Son dwell in us? How, then, does the
Father dwell in us? By referring to Lev.
26:12, from which Paul quoted, we find
that God promised to be in communion
with Israel, but there is nothing in the
passage to show his personal indwelling
in any one person. How does Christ
dwell in us? The passage above quoted
says, "Christ shall dwell in your hearts
by faith;" more correctly rendered, "the
faith" or *the gospel*. How does the
Spirit dwell in us? In Gal. 3:2, Paul
asks the Galatians: "Received ye the
Spirit by the works of the law, or by the
hearing of the faith?"—or the gospel.
The above Scriptures clearly teach that
when the words, thoughts and Spirit of
God are controlling in our lives, *God
dwells in us;* that when the gospel con-
trols us, *Christ dwells in us;* that when we

receive the gospel by the hearing of faith, *the Spirit dwells in us.*

Now, what reason has any man for declaring that the Spirit dwells in us in any other way, unless he can point to an explicit declaration of God's word defining and explaining that other way? This can not be done, for there is no such passage. "But," says one, "I do not have to depend upon the Word. I know it by my own consciousness." It is a principle as old as metaphysics that consciousness does not take cognizance of causes, but of effects. You may be conscious of an effect within you, but you can not be conscious of the cause that produced the effect. Suppose you are lying asleep on the ground; you are suddenly awakened by a severe pain in your lower limb; consciousness tells you that you are suffering pain, but it does not tell you what produced that pain. This must be decided by *reason* or *faith*. If you find a thorn in the grass where your limb was resting, *reason* says the thorn *stuck you;* if you find a bumblebee mashed in the grass, *reason* will say the insect *stung you;* or, if some one near you says a boy with a pin in his hand ran away from you, *faith* will say the boy *stuck you.* But in either case it was reason or faith that decided the cause of your pain. Now, when a man says, "I am conscious of the presence of the Holy Spirit within me," he simply means, "I am conscious of a *feeling* within me which I *have been taught* was caused by the Holy Spirit." If the man has been taught wrong, he assigns a *wrong cause* for the feeling. What is the feeling usually assigned for the presence of the Holy Spirit's personal indwelling? It is a feeling of joy, peace and love. But can not such feeling be excited by other causes? We know there are dozens of causes that will produce such feelings. In the absence of clear testimony, what right has any one to attribute such feeling to the personal presence of the Holy Spirit? A man is found murdered. The testimony shows that any one of a dozen men could have killed him. Is there an intelligent jury in the land that would convict any one of the men of being the murderer? What would you think of a jury that would render such a verdict?

"Well," says one, "what of the great numbers who pray for a 'Pentecostal revival'? Are they all wrong?" Not wrong in what they *want*, but wrong in *what they call it*. All that those pople desire, is to be filled with a *genuine revival of religious enthusiasm*. Their mistake is in calling it a "Pentecostal shower." A Pentecostal shower would lead every preacher under its influence to say, with the apostle Peter, to inquiring sinners: *"Repent, and be baptized every one of you in the name of Jesus Christ for the remission of sins."* This is what they are careful *not to say*. It is a clear evidence that the Spirit which guided Peter is not guiding them. I assert it to be a fact that everything that is claimed to be effected by a personal indwelling of the Spirit is as clearly accomplished by the Spirit acting through the word of God.

I do not wish to rest content with asserting that statement, but I wish to prove it. What are the things that might be accomplished by a direct personal indwelling of the Spirit in us?

1. He might give us faith.

But through the Word he does that. "So belief cometh of hearing, and hearing by the *word of Christ*" (Rom. 10:17).

2. He might enable us to enjoy a new birth.

But through the Word he does that. "Having been begotten again, not of corruptible seed, but of incorruptible, through the *word of God,* which liveth and abideth" (1 Pet. 1:23).

3. He might give us light.

But through the Word he does that. "The entrance of thy word giveth light" (Ps. 119:130).

4. He might give us wisdom.

But through the Word he does that. "But abide thou in the things which thou hast learned and hast been assured of, knowing of whom thou hast learned them; and that from a babe thou hast known the *sacred writings* which are able to *make thee wise* unto salvation through faith which is in Christ Jesus" (2 Tim. 3:14, 15). "The testimony of

Jehovah is sure, making wise the simple"
(Ps. 19:7).

5. He might convert us.

But he does that through the Word.
"The *law of Jehovah* is perfect, converting the soul" (Ps. 19:7).

6. He might open our eyes.

But he does that through the Word.
"The precepts of Jehovah are right, re-
joicing the heart; *The commandment* of
Jehovah is pure, enlightening the eyes"
(Ps. 19:8).

7. He might give us understanding.

But he does that through the Word.
"Through *thy precepts* I get understand-
ing: Therefore I hate every false way"
(Ps. 119:104).

8. He might quicken us.

But he does that through the Word.
"This is my comfort in my affliction; For
thy word hath quickened me" (Ps. 119:
50).

9. He might save us.

But he does that through the Word.
"Wherefore putting away all filthiness
and overflowing of wickedness, receive
with meekness the *implanted word*

which is able to save your souls'' (Jas. 1:21).

10. He might sanctify us.

But he does this through the Word. "Sanctify them in the truth: *thy word* is truth" (John 17:17).

11. He might purify us.

But he does that through the Word. "Seeing ye have purified your souls in your obedience to *the truth* unto unfeigned love of the brethren, love one another from the heart fervently" (1 Pet. 1:22).

12. He might cleanse us.

But he does that through the Word. "Already ye are clean because of *the word* which I have spoken unto you" (John 15:3).

13. He might make us free from sin.

But he does that through the Word. "But thanks be to God, that whereas ye were servants of sin, ye became obedient from the heart to that *form of teaching* whereunto ye were delivered; and being made free from sin, ye became servants of righteousness" (Rom. 6:17, 18).

14. He might impart a divine nature.

But he does that through the Word. "Whereby he hath granted unto us his precious and exceeding *great promises; that through these ye may become partakers of the divine nature,* having escaped from the corruption that is in the world by lust" (2 Pet. 1:4).

15. He might fit us for glory.

But he does that through the Word. "And now I commend you to God, and to *the word* of his grace, *which is able to build you up,* and to give you the inheritance among all them that are sanctified" (Acts 20:32).

16. He might strengthen us.

But he does that by his Word. Strengthen me according to thy word" (Ps. 119:28).

In the above cases we have covered all the conceivable things a direct indwelling Spirit could do for one, and have also shown that all these things the Spirit does through the word of God. It is not claimed that a direct indwelling of the Spirit makes any new revelations, adds any new reasons or offers any new

125

motives than are found in the word of God. Of what use, then, would a direct indwelling Spirit be? God makes nothing in vain. We are necessarily, therefore, led to the conclusion that, in dealing with his children to-day, God deals with them in the same psychological way that he deals with men in inducing them to become children. This conclusion is strengthened by the utter absence of any test by which we could know the Spirit dwells in us, if such were the case.

WHAT THE SPIRIT DOES FOR CHRISTIANS.

1. *He is active in our birth.* "Jesus answered, Verily, verily, I say unto thee, Except one be born of water and the Spirit, he cannot enter into the kingdom of God" (John 3:5).

Here is a distinct statement of a radical change, so radical as to be likened to a new birth in order that we may enter the kingdom of God. What is it that is born? Christ says, "A man." But what is a man? We regard a man as having a mind, a heart and a body. There is no perfect man where any of these elements is lacking. If, therefore, a man is born again, he must be born in mind, in heart, in body. How is this birth accomplished? Let us see what the Word says. "But as many as received him, to them gave he the right to become children of God, even to them that believe on his name: who were born, not of blood, nor of the will of the flesh, nor of the will of man, *but of God*" (John 1:12, 13).

God gives all things—sometimes directly, sometimes through an agent. The Holy Spirit is the agent. "Born of water and the Spirit." But an agent often works through an instrument. What is the instrument? The word of God. "Seeing ye have purified your souls in your obedience to the truth unto unfeigned love of the brethren, love one another from the heart fervently; having been begotten again, not of corruptible seed, but of incorruptible, *through the word of God,* which liveth and abideth" (1 Pet. 1:22, 23).

How can the word of God accomplish the new birth? By the only way that words can accomplish any change—by being heard, understood, and influencing the life. The Holy Spirit puts himself into the words that contain his motives, actions and promises. How can this be done? Just as man does it. Years ago the prophet Mohammed put his spirit into the words, ''There is one God, and Mohammed is his prophet.'' When a man reads these words and believes and acts upon them, the spirit of Mohammed enters into that man and dwells there as long as the man continues true to those words. The only way to take the spirit of Mohammed out of those words is to transpose them so they will not say what he said.

George Washington put his spirit into the sentence, ''United we stand, divided we fall.'' As long as the American people are true to the above words, the spirit of George Washington will live in them. But make the same words read, ''Divided we stand, united we fall,'' and the spirit of Washington is removed from them. The only way to take the Spirit of God from the word of God is to add to, take from or transpose the Word so it will not say what the Spirit *said in it*.

"Well," says one, "if we are born of the Spirit operating through the Word, must we not understand all the Word in order that we may be born again?" No, the apostle limits the part of the Word we must understand in verse 25 of this same chapter: "This is the word which by *the gospel* is preached unto you." Let us now endeavor to learn how the gospel produces this change. How is the mind born again? In order to learn this we must understand what is the normal condition of the mind of the unregenerate. In general we may say it is in a state of *unbelief*. Now, the proclamation of the great facts of the death, burial and resurrection of Christ according to the Scriptures will break up that condition of unbelief and produce a conviction of the truth of the gospel. When the mind is changed from a state of unbelief to one of hearty belief the birth of the mind is complete. But the mind is only a part of man. The heart must be born again. What is the normal state of the unregenerate heart? It is one of either *indifference* or *hatred*. The latter is the former fully ripened. It is said that Voltaire carried a seal ring upon which were engraved the words, "Crush the wretch," and every time he sealed a letter he impressed his spirit of hatred upon that letter. Now, the gospel sets forth the love of God in Christ and the loveliness of Christ's sacrifice for us in such a manner as to change the indifferent or malignant heart into one of supreme love to Christ. When the heart has thus been changed from hatred to love it is born again. But man has also a body, and upon this spirit can not act. If the body is to be born again, some element must be used that can act upon the body. Hence our Saviour says, "born of water and the Spirit," because water can act upon the body. Now, the only use of water in the new birth is in the act of baptism. All scholars of note in the religious world agree that Christ's use of water in the new birth has reference to baptism. Paul also speaks of "having our hearts sprinkled from an evil conscience and our bodies washed in pure water.'' Thus, with mind and heart changed by the Spirit through the gospel, and the body solemnly consecrated to God in baptism, the entire man is born again. This is all accomplished by the Spirit of God working *in and through the gospel*.

2. Another work of the Spirit is to *''bear witness with our spirits that we are children of God, and if children, then heirs''* (Rom. 8:16). It does not say, ''bear witness *to* our spirits,'' but *''with* our spirits.''* Many people gauge the witness of the Spirit by feelings within themselves. If they feel good, it is evidence to them of the Spirit's testimony, but they frequently feel bad also; whose testimony is that? The testimony of the Spirit should be clear testimony, and not fluctuating; it should be in words, and not in feelings. Feelings, impressions and emotions come and go like the waves of the sea, but words remain forever the same. ''Heaven and earth shall pass away, but my word shall not pass away,'' saith the Lord. The idea of the conscious testimony of the Spirit is not sustained

10   131

by either the word of God nor a correct psychology. It is the testimony of meta-physicians, from Sir William Hamilton down to the writer, that consciousness does not take cognizance of causes, but effects. Feelings are effects and not causes. Consciousness tells us when we feel good or bad, but it does not tell us what makes us feel good or bad. When a man has been taught that a certain feeling in the heart is produced by a certain agency, his faith and reason may decide that that agency produced the feeling, but consciousness has nothing whatever to do with *the cause* of the feeling. Likewise, a certain feeling in the heart may be attributed to the Spirit because one has been taught that the Spirit will produce such a feeling, but consciousness can not trace that feeling to the Spirit himself. A man should feel right because he knows he is right, and not know he is right because he feels right.

In deciding whether we be children of God, we have two witnesses: first, the Spirit himself, and, second, our spirit. The Spirit testifies as to who is a child of God; our spirits testify as to what we are. If our spirits testify that we are the character which the Spirit says belongs to a child of God, then we have the testimony of the Spirit himself bearing witness with our spirits that we are children of God. The testimony of the Spirit, in the nature of the case, must be general. He testifies that whosoever believes in Christ, repents of his sins, and is baptized into him, is a child of God. This is the whole of his testimony. Your spirit, likewise, must bear witness to your position on all of these points.

No one but your own spirit can testify that you believe in Christ; you may profess to, and the whole world may believe that you do, but your own spirit knows that you are a hypocrite in making the profession. Likewise, no one can testify but your own spirit that you have repented; you may make professions of repentance, and the world may believe you thoroughly sincere, but your own spirit may tell you that your profession is false. In a similar manner, no one but your own spirit can testify that you have been bap-

tized; your father and mother may say
so, the church record may so testify, and
yet it is possible for them to be mistaken.
To be certain you are a child of God you
must have the testimony of your own
spirit that you believe, that you have repented and that you have been baptized.
If, in the judgment day, God should ask
such people, "Have you obeyed me in the
act of Christian baptism?" they would
not have the testimony of their spirit
that they had so obeyed; they would have
to fall back upon the church record or
that of their father and mother. Others
may be satisfied with such testimony, but,
as for myself, if I did not have the testimony of my own spirit that I had obeyed
the Lord in Christian baptism, I would
obtain that testimony before the going
down of the sun.

"Well," says one, "is that all the witness of the Spirit mentioned by the apostle?" Yes, that is all; absolutely and
unqualifiedly all. What more can you desire? "Well," says another, "I want
something more than the mere word; I
want to be saved like the thief on the

cross." How do you know that the thief
on the cross was saved? "Oh, the Bible
says he was." True, but that is the testimony of the "mere word"; so you have
as much testimony to your own salvation
as you have for the salvation of the thief
on the cross, and it would be impossible
for you to have any more. Suppose the
Lord were to come down and take you up
bodily and set you down before his throne
in heaven, and, in the presence of all the
angels and archangels, say to you: "My
child, your sins are all forgiven."
"Now," says one, "that would be testimony indeed." Yes, it would be testimony, but no more testimony than you
have in the word of God now; you would
then have only the testimony of the
"mere word" of God that you were forgiven. All such criticisms arise out of
infidelity as to the truthfulness of God's
word.

3. *The Spirit maketh intercession for
us.* This is not a work done in us nor
upon us, but is something done for us
before the throne of God. We can not
dogmatize as to *how* the Spirit maketh

intercession, but Paul says he does it *"according to the will of God."* This is a fact that appeals to *our faith* and not to our Christian *experience*. It "can not be uttered." We can rest upon it and draw comfort from it as a child draws strength from its mother's breast. We can also draw comfort from the fact that Christ "ever liveth to make intercession for us," though we have no knowledge as to *how* he does it.

4. Another work of the Spirit is to *"change us from glory to glory."* "But we all, with unveiled face, reflecting as a mirror the glory of the Lord, are transformed into the same image from glory to glory, even as from the Lord the Spirit" (2 Cor. 3:18). The figure used here by the apostle is taken from the process of mirror-making among the ancients. They hadn't the glass mirrors of our day, but a mirror of highly polished metal. A piece of coarse metal would be placed upon a stone and the workmen would begin to polish it; at first it made no reflection at all, but when polished for awhile would give a distorted

136

and perverted reflection; but in the process of polishing, that reflection would grow clearer and clearer, when finally a man could behold his face in it perfectly reflected. And so with us. When taken into the great spiritual laboratory of Christianity we are blocks in the rough, but in the polishing process of the church and spiritual surroundings we begin to reflect the image of our Master, and when we have completed the work, we reflect him as perfectly as a human being can. Take, for illustration, the brothers Peter and John. At first they were called Boanerges, sons of thunder; they wanted to call down fire from heaven to destroy men who differed from them; but in the great laboratory of the Christian life they grew more and more Christlike, transformed by the Spirit of God, until at last we see the old apostle John at Ephesus, beautified and ennobled, sitting in his chair and lifting up trembling hands, and saying to the young disciples: "Little children, love one another, for love is of God." We see the transforming power of the spiritual atmosphere of the

137

church and the Christian life upon human nature. Christian, with this illustration before you, how can you excuse yourself for keeping out of the spiritual atmosphere of God, for staying away from the communion and the spiritual convocation of God's people? Is it a burden and a duty to attend the house of God, or is it a pleasure gladly and joyfully anticipated? When you rise on the Lord's Day morning, do you say, "Must I go to church to-day?" or do you say:

"You may sing of the beauty of mountain and dale,
 The water of streamlet and the flowers of the vale,
 But the place most delightful this earth can afford,
 Is the place of devotion, the house of the Lord"?

5. The last work of the Spirit which the word of God mentions is the *"quickening of our mortal bodies."* "But if the Spirit of him that raised up Jesus from the dead dwell in you, he that raised up Christ Jesus from the dead shall quicken your mortal bodies through his Spirit that dwelleth in you" (Rom. 8:11). This Spirit which has ever been with us, watching over us, will never leave us until he raises our bodies from the dead

and fashions our vile bodies like unto the glorious body of our Lord. It matters much where we now live; it matters little where and how we die. Our bodies may be buried in the unfathomed caves of ocean; they may lie upon some mountain-peak or be placed in a crowded cemetery of some great city. No stone may mark our resting-place, no friend may be able to find the spot and place a flower of love upon it; but that abiding-place is known to the infinite Spirit of God, and from our ashes he will quicken our bodies and present us faultless before the throne of God.

> "I know not where His isles may lift
>   Their fronded palms in air:
> I only know I can not drift
>   Beyond His love and care."

We have not space in this chapter to notice other than the principal passages which refer to the work of the Spirit as it relates to Christians, but in the five above mentioned there is no hint that he does anything in us other than through the instrumentality of the gospel, and there are no other passages that teach a direct work upon us more clearly than those mentioned.

There are many passages that trace the blessed and glorious work of the Spirit in us and through us, but they all confirm the clear statement quoted from the *Sunday School Times* that he works *mediately*, and not *immediately*.

X

THE PARTING WORD

BLASPHEMY against the Spirit. This is a subject that is intensely interesting to many people. They imagine that in some way unknown to themselves they *may* have committed this act, and it causes them great concern. I will say that such people need have no alarm. The man who has actually committed this sin *never* feels any alarm about it. He is the last man to feel concern over it. By reading the twelfth chapter of Matthew the reader can obtain a clear view of this sin. Jesus was being hounded by the Pharisees, who had determined to procure his death at all hazards. They were watching, exaggerating and criticizing everything he did.

He went on a Sabbath day through the field of corn and his disciples plucked and ate some of the corn. There was an immediate outcry of "The Sabbath is violated." Again, Jesus healed the man with a withered hand and the Pharisees went out and held a council to plan his destruction. Again, there was brought to him a man possessed of a devil, rendering him blind and dumb. Jesus healed him by casting out the devil, so that he "both saw and heard." Casting out devils had always been regarded by the Jews as a direct work of the Spirit of God. The people are amazed, and proclaimed him the Son of David, or the Messiah. The Pharisees could not deny the fact, but they said: "He does it by Beelzebub, the prince of devils."

These three incidents show a disposition on their part to deliberately reject all testimony contrary to their plan to compass his death. They had rendered their verdict in advance and were not open to conviction, no matter *what* testimony might be offered. Jesus tells them that if he casts out devils by Beelzebub, then Satan is divided against himself. "But if I by the Spirit of God cast out devils, then is the kingdom of God come

upon me" (Matt. 12:28). *"Therefore
I say unto you, Every sin and blasphemy
shall be forgiven unto men: but the blasphemy against the Spirit shall not be forgiven. And whosoever shall speak a word
against the Son of man, it shall be forgiven him: but whosoever shall speak
against the Holy Spirit, it shall not be
forgiven him, neither in this world, nor
in that which is to come"* (Matt. 12:31,
32). That these men had committed, or
were in great danger of committing, this
blasphemy is evident from the caution
uttered above.

When a man to-day reaches the com-
prehensive state of mind that he is going
to reject Jesus *over any and all evidence,*
he has gone into the house, shut and
locked the door and thrown away the
key. God can not reach him. Such a man
will be let alone by the Spirit of God.
That Paul understood this condition to be
unpardonable, we read in Heb. 6:4-6:
"But as touching those who were once
enlightened, and tasted of the heavenly
gift, and were made partakers of the Holy
Spirit, and tasted the good word of God,

143

and the powers of the age to come, and then fall away, it is impossible to renew them again unto repentance; seeing they *crucify to themselves the Son of God afresh,* and put him to an open shame." Paul says it is impossible to renew such a one to repentance. Why? *"Seeing they crucify to themselves the Son of God afresh."* That is, they have reached the same state of mind the Pharisees had who *crucified him the first time.* Men can commit that same act to-day, but when they do it they lose all concern regarding the consequences. As long as one has concern, he may rest assured that he has not blasphemed the Holy Spirit.

The Fruits of the Spirit. I have not treated this passage hitherto, because I do not understand the apostle to be referring to the Holy Spirit, but to man's spirit. In this fifth chapter of Galatians the apostle divides man into two domains, one of the flesh and another of the spirit. He says: "The flesh lusteth against the Spirit, and the Spirit against the flesh: for these are contrary the one to the

144

other: that ye *may not do the things that ye would*" (Gal. 5:17). It is impossible to imagine "the flesh" preventing the Holy Spirit from doing "the things he would." It is also impossible to conceive that the Holy Spirit is lusting against man's flesh. But we all recognize that there is a terrible conflict between man's flesh and *his spirit*. These are contrary the one to the other and lust against each other. When man's flesh triumphs over his spirit, certain works are inevitable which Paul enumerates. When the Spirit (in man) dominates the flesh, then certain "fruits of the Spirit" appear. They are the fruits of man's spiritual nature triumphing over his fleshly nature. The same contrast is set forth in Galatians, chapter 6, where it speaks of sowing to the flesh and to the Spirit. How can any man sow to the Holy Spirit? Paul describes the same conflict in the seventh chapter of Romans. I think that the spirit (of man) can be aided by the Holy Spirit in its battle against the flesh, but the "fruits" mentioned are of man's spirit and not the Holy Spirit.

The Spirit of God at Work To-day.
Says one, "Is not the Spirit actively at
work in the world to-day?" Of course he
is. It is not a question of *what* he is
doing, but *how* he is doing it. The religious world is pretty generally agreed that
the Spirit is pleading with the world of
the unsaved through the motives and in-
ducements of the gospel, the moral truth
which appeals to the intellect and heart
of the unconverted to turn to God and be
saved; that all the saving power of God
is found in Christ and the gospel which
reveals him; that God will not go beyond
the cross of Christ to save any man. It
is Christ "who was made unto us wisdom
from God, and righteousness and sanctification, and redemption: that, according
as it is written, He that glorieth, let him
glory in the Lord." All that is necessary
for wisdom, righteousness, sanctification
and redemption—and that is all we need
—is found in Christ. This being so, we
need no other power but gospel power in
our attempts to become children of God
or to live as children of God. We get
into confusion when we try to obtain some

146

other and more direct power. We are led into a dependence upon our feelings, which are unreliable.

Bishop J. H. Vincent, than whom stands no higher in the Northern M. E. Church, aptly states the whole matter thus: "There are people who put stress on sentiment and emotion in religion. If they 'feel good,' they have no doubt as to their present security and their acceptance with God. These people covet moods and states of feeling. They revel in songs and prayers and hallelujahs. The thrill of sentiment and the warm currents of emotion are 'the all and in all' of religion. Such saints forget that mere mental exhilaration and good feeling may coexist with carnal hearts, selfish aims, and utter worldliness of temper." His brethren will scarcely accuse the Bishop of not believing in "heartfelt religion," and yet they used to strongly accuse us of denying it, because we plead for the testimony of the Book rather than the testimony of feeling.

We get into the same confusion when we attempt to fall back upon some inward power, independent of God's word, in living the Christian life. The writer has known many good, honest people that claimed to have an inward monitor to lead them, who at the same time would reject the clear teaching of God's word. The Spirit of God never led any man to contradict *the Word* which he has so clearly revealed. The whole Christian life is a life of faith. *It begins, continues and ends in faith.* "God is no respecter of persons, but in every nation he that *fears God and works righteousness* is accepted of him." "The sword of the Spirit" is "the word of God."

www.ingramcontent.com/pod-product-compliance
Lightning Source LLC
LaVergne TN
LVHW011239080426
835509LV00005B/556